7 Creative Models for Community Ministry

JOY F. SKJEGSTAD

JUDSON PRESS
PUBLISHERS SINCE 1824
VALLEY FORGE, PA

7 Creative Models for Community Ministry

Judson Press has made every effort to trace the ownership of all quotes. In the event of a question arising from the use of a quote, we regret any error made and will be pleased to make the necessary correction in future printings and editions of this book.

Bible quotations in this volume are from the New Revised Standard Version Bible, copyright © 1989, Division of Christian Education of the National Council of the Churches of Christ in the United States of America. Used by permission. All rights reserved.

Bible quotations marked NASB are from the New American Standard Bible, © 1960, 1962, 1963, 1968, 1971, 1972, 1973, 1975, 1977, 1995 by The Lockman Foundation. Used by permission.

Bible quotations marked NIV are from the HOLY BIBLE, NEW INTERNATIONAL VERSION®. NIV®. Copyright © 1973, 1978, 1984, 2011 by Biblica, Inc.™ Used by permission. All rights reserved worldwide.

Interior design by Crystal Devine.
Cover design by Wendy Ronga, Hampton Design Group.

Library of Congress Cataloging-in-Publication data

Skjegstad, Joy.
  7 creative models for community ministry / Joy F. Skjegstad. -- First edition
    pages cm
  ISBN 978-0-8170-1730-9 (pbk. : alk. paper) 1. Communities--Religious aspects--Christianity. 2. Church work. I. Title. II. Title: Seven creative models for community ministry.
  BV625.S555 2013
  253'.7--dc23
                        2013004150

Printed in the U.S.A.
First Edition, 2013.

For my Dad, Arnold E. Skjegstad (1920–2009),
who loved the church and his fellow believers
with a dedication that I can only hope to emulate.

Contents

Acknowledgments

I wrote this book during what ended up being a difficult year for our family. I am indebted to the people who helped me in the production of this book, but also to those who prayed for our family and showed us friendship during a difficult time.

I have knowledge on the topics in this book because, along the way, several congregations were willing to give me opportunities to take leadership in community ministry and try new things (and fail at some of them). Serving as a staff member of Park Avenue United Methodist Church in South Minneapolis and of Sanctuary Covenant Church in North Minneapolis provided me with amazing on-the-job experience as I worked side-by-side with people who had worked and lived in the community for years. In more recent years, a number of my consulting clients have allowed me to see the best of community ministry, teaching me what it really takes to make a difference. There are many, but I wanted to particularly acknowledge The Banyan Community, Redeemer Center for Life, First Covenant Church of St. Paul, Messiah Lutheran Church, Bethel University's King Family Child Development Center, and the Union Gospel Mission.

I am also grateful to the many people who allowed me to interview them for the book (all of them are listed at the end of this Acknowledgments). People I talked to were willing to share their stories and were honest about the challenges and frustrations of doing good work in the community. Colleen Beebe and Kim Loontjer read my initial manuscript and provided insightful comments.

My editor at Judson Press, Rebecca Irwin-Diehl, shaped a rough manuscript into something smooth, and challenged me to include more biblical references throughout the book.

I am blessed with a group of loyal friends who pray for me and encourage me all the time—and who have a high tolerance for being blasted with angst and frustration over coffee and on phone calls! My thanks to Linda, Nancy, Nora, Tessa, Marie, Janice, Mary, Dave and Diane, Holly and Joe, Paul and Libby, and Vanessa and Mark. Many other people at our church, Messiah Episcopal, also prayed for me during the process of writing this book. Special thanks to the Prayer and Healing Team at Messiah and our Rector, John Newton, who greeted me at the door of the church one weekday with: "Oh, I have just been praying for you. Would you like a cup of tea?"

And finally, and most importantly, I need to acknowledge the contributions of my family. My children, Ethan and Julia, gave up time with their mom so I could write this book, and were constantly saying, "You can do it, Mom!" And my husband, Brad Schrag, supported me with his love, encouragement, and willingness to pick up the slack around the house. Brad, you always take the leap with me into new adventures happily and with good humor. Really, I couldn't do it without you.

Thanks to the following people who allowed me to interview them for this book. If I interviewed you and failed to include you on this list, please accept both my gratitude and apologies.

Lisa Adams, Crossroads Covenant Church, Woodbury, MN
Rev. Sally Bingham, Interfaith Power and Light, San Francisco, CA
Cathy Brechtelsbauer, St. Mark's Lutheran Church, Sioux Falls, SD
Ann Carlson, The Dignity Center at Hennepin Avenue United
    Methodist Church, Minneapolis, MN
Rev. Jay Carlson, Holy Trinity Lutheran Church, Minneapolis, MN
Rev. Kelly Chatman, Redeemer Lutheran Church and Redeemer
    Center for Life, Minneapolis, MN
Rev. David Eckert, Drexel Hill United Methodist Church, Drexel
    Hill, PA
Rev. Chris Enstad, Elim Lutheran Church, Robbinsdale, MN

Rev. Cyndi Gavin, St. John's United Church of Christ, Aurora, IL

Sue Hewitt, LINC Twin Cities, Minneapolis/St. Paul, MN

Michael Hitch, The Restoration Initiative for Culture and Community, New Orleans, LA

Rev. Mike Hotz, Christ Presbyterian Church, Edina, MN

Bishop Richard Howell, Shiloh Temple, Minneapolis, MN

Denise Kesanen, RiverWorks, Riverwood Covenant Church, Rockford, MN

Alison Killeen, Joint Religious Legislative Coalition, Minneapolis, MN

Rev. Craig Lewis, Evangelical Lutheran Church of America, Minneapolis, MN

Rev. Jeff Lindsay, Colonial Church of Edina, Edina, MN

Jen Lindwall, formerly of Church of the Open Door, Maple Grove, MN

Matt McDermott, Congregations Organized for a New Connecticut, New Haven, CT

Meghan Olsen-Biebighauser, Holy Trinity Lutheran Church, Minneapolis, MN

Pat Peterson, Fairview Health Services, Minneapolis, MN

Dr. Raymond Rivera, Latino Pastoral Action Center, Bronx, NY

Ruston Seaman, New Vision Renewable Energy, based in Philippi, WV

Rev. John Sommerville, City Church, Minneapolis, MN

Rev. Joe Sutton, Believers in Christ, Minneapolis, MN

Marilu Thomas, formerly of Redeemer Center for Life, Minneapolis, MN

Sue Timmerman, St. Michael's Lutheran Church, Bloomington, MN

Rev. Sue Tjornehoj, formerly of the Minneapolis Area Synod of the ELCA

Pastor Sandra Unger, The Lift CDC, St. Paul, MN

Lori Wagner, St. Michael's Lutheran Church, Bloomington, MN

Tammy Walhof, Bread for the World, Minneapolis, MN

Lisa Welter, Eagle Brook Church, 5 locations in the Twin Cities, MN

Mark Wilkening, formerly of Youthworks Foundation, Minneapolis, MN

Craig Wong, Grace Urban Ministries, San Francisco, CA

PART ONE

Getting Started

Finding a Fit between Church and Community

This book is for you if you have already decided that your church should get more engaged with your community and you need to know what to do next. Maybe you and others at your church have had an experience where the needs and issues of your community hit you hard, and you could see that you had to do something. Sometimes churches get shocked into action—by violence or tragedy in the neighborhood, by the increasing number of hungry people asking for food, or by some other dire situation.

Sometimes the community nudges the church forward—residents have a passion to start something new, and your congregation is drawn into the excitement of a new vision for the community. A church I worked for once was drawn into a new movement in the neighborhood to develop after-school programs—it was as if we were swept along with the tide of great ideas in the community!

Or maybe you and other like-minded people in your church have come to realize that it is time to get outside your walls. When I was on staff at Park Avenue United Methodist Church in Minneapolis, I knew God was at work when different people who didn't know each other would approach me with the same idea for new ministry. We started a legal clinic that way, staffed by volunteer lawyers from our church.

Maybe you have come to this place by reading a good book on the topic of church serving community, such as *The Externally*

Focused Church by Rick Rusaw and Eric Swanson (Group, 2004), or *Learning Mission, Living Mission: Churches That Work* by Glynis LaBarre (Judson, 2012), or you are in a church revitalization process that has community outreach as a focus.

However it is that you have arrived at the vision for greater community engagement, I hope this book can help you see what to do next. The book is focused on seven models for how community ministry can be delivered and structured when connected to the local church, identifying the pros and cons of each model and how your church might take steps to implement each one. I have seen each of the models be effective in a variety of church settings, so I can't advocate one model over another. You need to choose a model based on what is good for your community and what is suitable or beneficial for your church.

What Is Community Ministry?

"Community" can be defined in a number of different ways. In an urban setting, the community context is often defined as one neighborhood or even part of one neighborhood. In rural areas, your community might be your town or several towns or even your county. Suburbs might define community according to a subdivision or a school district. I am defining community ministry as *any effort your church makes to connect with people and institutions outside the four walls of your church.*

Many congregations have people from the community among their members, so the line between community and church isn't a fixed one. Your neighborhood-based church members may have some of the same issues and concerns as the people from outside your church who live in the community, so you may need to do some "internal" ministry to help them meet their needs. For example, if your church decides to work on the foreclosure crisis in your community by helping fund mortgage payments, it is important to notice that there are people in your own congregation who are in the same boat and to help them as well. This book is not primarily about this kind of internal ministry—my focus here is more on the process of getting outside the church to build new ministry.

Seven Models for Community Ministry

Model 1   Donate Goods or Money
Collecting and sending money or material goods to aid a cause that your congregation cares about. You might collect things like school supplies, books, or food.

Model 2   Mobilize Volunteers
Sending volunteers from your church to work with a nonprofit or other organization in your community, like the Boys and Girls Clubs or Habitat for Humanity, for example.

Model 3   Partner with Other Organizations
A more full-fledged partnership with a nonprofit or other type of group in your community. Some options include sending volunteers, donating money or items, planning and delivering programs together, and sharing space.

Model 4   Advocate around Public Policy
Working together as a congregation to advocate for public policy change on a particular issue, such as affordable housing or funding for public schools.

Model 5   Engage in Community Organizing
Your church working side by side with community residents and other community organizations to produce change that gets at the "root" of community issues. This model might include actions like picketing or boycotting to address housing discrimination.

Model 6   Develop a Ministry Program
Developing your own program from the ground up—your church has the vision for the program and develops a plan, staffs the program with paid staff or volunteers, secures other resources like space and equipment, and is responsible for managing the program.

Model 7   Create a Church-Based Nonprofit
Starting a separate 501(c)3 nonprofit organization connected to your church that would serve as an umbrella for community ministry programs.

Hybrids Are Possible

Part Two outlines seven models for community ministry. I recommend starting with one model, but as you gain experience in ministry or grow your program, you may decide that you would like to add one or more additional models to the ministry mix. Many churches blend two or more ministry models together—these are "hybrids," and I have noted a number of these throughout the book in the case studies of churches. For example, community ministry work on public education might evolve along these lines:

1. We start by collecting school supplies for the local public school.
2. Then we mobilize church members into the schools, serving as volunteer reading tutors.
3. Then we form a more full-fledged partnership with the school, helping with events, sending people to participate in the Parent Teacher Organization or on the Site-Based Council, or helping connect the school to new partnerships and grant funding.
4. Then we decide to work on public policy issues related to public education, like a school funding referendum or proposed cuts in school nutrition programs.

Know that you have choices. Many churches come with pre-conceived ideas about what community ministry looks like and how it is structured. Some think that starting their own program at the church or forming a church-based nonprofit is a must. But it may not be the right fit if you are working in a community already overloaded with organizations and programs. Perhaps you need to partner with a nearby community organization instead, such as a shelter for the homeless or a job training center.

Other communities may have a lot of willing volunteers but no organization or program capable of mobilizing them. That is why part of the process is exploring what needs and resources already exist—and how your church might be part of bringing the two together.

When I worked on the North Side of Minneapolis, for example, I was shocked during our community listening process when residents kept saying that more youth programming was needed in the community. Many organizations were already providing programs for youth! But people said certain geographic pockets of the neighborhood were totally unserved by existing programs. Furthermore, there were few programs for middle school youth. This gave us some clear direction in how to shape the community-based youth programs that we offered through our church.

The Place Where the Church and the Community Kiss Each Other

My hope is that you will find a way to do community ministry that is good for the community *and* good for the people in your church. Psalm 85:10 (NASB) says, "Lovingkindness and truth have met together; righteousness and peace have kissed each other." I encourage you to find the place where the church and community can kiss each other—where real needs are being met, relationships are being formed, and people's gifts are being used in ministry.

You find that place by getting out and meeting your neighbors (see pages 11–27) so that your ministry is designed to respond to actual community needs and is launched in partnership with people and organizations in the community. Taking the time to meet people and listen to them will help you to build on assets in the community and the work that is already being done. Even if all you do is meet the neighbors and never implement any of the seven models described in this book, your congregation will be changed in the process.

My own ideas and the way I do ministry have been completely transformed by knowing people in the neighborhood. It's one thing to look at a demographic report on paper; it's another thing entirely to be able to call one of the "mothers" of the community in North Minneapolis to get her perspective and to find out what is really going on. Sitting on committees, attending neighborhood association meetings, going to community events, and inviting your neighbors in for coffee—these are all ways to meet the neighbors, and the impact on your life will be significant.

Ministry That Is Good for Everyone Involved

Finding the fit between your church and the community is important, because it is possible to do ministry in a way that is good for the community and damaging to the people in your church—or conversely, to do ministry that the church revels in but that ultimately fails the community.

Sometimes congregations get excited about serving the community and bite off too much, putting too small a group of church members in charge of too large of a ministry. People get burned out and quit and may be reticent to sign up to volunteer again. I have known a few people over the years who left the church entirely because the burden they were given to carry as a volunteer was just too heavy for them.

Other times the issue is not the number of volunteers but the preparation for the task. Church members get mobilized into a situation that they have not been prepared for—for example, crossing the cultural divide or working with a challenging population of people without first being trained. I caution about this because sometimes visionary church leaders have the community clearly in focus but not their church members. So as you consider how to move forward into the community, be sure you are tending to the people in your church. (Model 2 describes how you can equip volunteers before you send them out, providing training, mentoring, and support that will help them have a good experience.)

The other side of the fit between church and community is to do your ministry in a way that benefits the community rather than hurting it. The danger of hurting your community with well-intentioned ministry efforts has been written about at length by a number of authors.[1] Sometimes church leaders will choose a project that is easy, just for the ease of it, without considering the impact on the community. For example, short-term projects or events might make your church members feel good but may have little real impact on the community over the long term. For example, a church might send volunteers to a neighborhood cleanup event—a one-time effort involving raking leaves and picking up trash. There is nothing wrong with cleaning up, but by itself, it is unlikely to make an ongoing difference in the neighborhood or help your congregation build deep relationships in the community.

Dropping into the community quickly and then exiting could offend community residents and may give them the impression that your church is just like everyone else—not in it for the long haul. In many communities, residents have seen do-gooders come and go over and over again, so they are skeptical about the intentions of people who show up just once in a while. For that reason, if you choose Model 1 (Donate Goods or Money), I recommend doing it on a consistent basis, perhaps sending volunteers as well (Model 2) so that you can learn and build relationships.

It is also possible to damage the community if you come to ministry with the wrong attitude. In my experience, relating to someone with love and humility and treating them like they are a treasure is the ministry. Anything else you do (connect people to jobs, teach reading, serve meals) is just gravy compared to that. So be humble about how much you may actually be able to help someone. Don't judge. Listen to the people's stories, even if parts of the stories are challenging for you to hear.

The best community ministry programs I have seen acknowledge giftedness within the community. Great power comes from looking out into the community and seeing ideas, dreams, capacity, and experience instead of simply needs, problems, and dysfunction. One church has a large community garden and relies on neighborhood residents to teach kids how to prepare the vegetables they have been tending all summer, using old family recipes shared by the residents. All of this cooking know-how within just a few blocks of the church is an asset that is being used to minister to young people.

Be Faithful and Keep Trying

My hope is that after reading this book, you will want to try meeting the neighbors, connecting with your community in new ways, and forming new partnerships or ministry programs. Lots of risks and dangers are involved in doing this work, but I believe we have to try. Do some reading, some praying, and some planning, and then get out there and try.

And it is essential to keep trying, because good community ministry requires flexibility and a willingness to admit mistakes. If what you have done so far has not worked out so well, take a step back and ask some of the hard questions about capacity, vision, and community needs. And then keep trying. You may need to try a different approach or model, enlist new partners, or do more work inside your church to tap into the vision and the gifts there. Some of the largest and most successful community ministry programs around the United States (the ones highlighted often in books) began small and grew out of initial failures. They grew into what they are today because leaders were willing to keep learning and growing and moving forward despite initial setbacks.

Communities all across the United States are depending on the church to be a good neighbor—whether that means donating food, tutoring children, starting a preschool or homeless shelter, or partnering with the local health clinic. We have to be faithful and keep trying.

NOTE

1. See, for example, Robert Lupton, *Toxic Charity* (New York: HarperCollins, 2011); and Steve Corbett and Brian Fikkert, *When Helping Hurts: How to Alleviate Poverty without Hurting the Poor . . . and Yourself* (Chicago: Moody, 2009).

Meeting the Neighbors: Ten Ways to Connect with the Community

The best community ministry efforts arise out of a close connection with neighbors. When you actually know the people of your community, you can better understand needs and issues, as well as the many gifts and assets present there. Out of these relationships, relevant ministry can arise. For example, you won't want to start another youth program when it's affordable housing that people actually need (and there are already ten youth programs operating nearby). Knowing your neighbors can also create a partnership in ministry—it breaks down the walls between those who minister and those who are being ministered to. After a while, you are doing ministry together.

Things I Learned from the Neighbors

I have had the privilege of running two church-based nonprofits and am now a consultant with a number of ministry groups, so I have been engaged in a number of listening processes. A listening process, as described in detail later in this chapter, is meeting and listening to the people in your community through a variety of means, including engaging in one-on-one interviews, participating in community groups, attending events, and "hanging out" at places in the community. Through listening processes I have facilitated, I have talked with youth; parents; neighborhood residents;

and participants in affordable housing programs, health clinics, drug treatment programs, and a number of other initiatives.

Here are a few things I have learned by meeting the neighbors:

- The kids in the community didn't want another basketball program; they wanted jobs.
- Dozens of adults in the neighborhood were already engaged in informal youth programming on their blocks, helping children with homework, playing sports with them, and mentoring them.
- The homeless people really wanted milk (no one else provided it) and a place to make free phone calls.
- One community had a concentration of people who knew how to do car and home repairs.
- The neighborhood association needed someone to help them plan and implement events.

The comments above helped the churches and organizations involved shape their programming to respond to real needs in the community and to build on community assets. By listening carefully, you will discover similar insights that are helpful in framing your community ministry.

Skipping the Listening Process Can Be Tempting

Skipping the listening process can be tempting, and I am always surprised by the number of churches that skip over this step entirely. It is faster to plan programming without it, because listening takes time—more time than just plotting out what is already in your head. If your church is on a deadline for getting plans completed and the calendar filled out, it can be hard to say, "Wait! We really need to talk to the community about this first!"

Another reason churches skip the listening step is that it can be intimidating to meet people you don't know, particularly if your church is in a community where the people in the neighborhood are very different from the people in your church. Communicating with someone from a different ethnic, cultural, socioeconomic, or religious background can be challenging, particularly if you have never done it before. I can assure you that it is possible to learn how to do this, speaking as a white woman from Duluth, Minnesota, who is continuing to learn how to connect with African immigrants, Hmong and Karen people, Latino people from many nations, African Americans, Muslims and Jews, and people who live in poverty (frequently all present in my local grocery store at the same time!).

Another barrier can be the need to admit that more input is needed—that we don't have everything figured out yet. Saying, "We need more information and more people engaged before we proceed" forces us to realize that we aren't the experts we thought we were. Particularly for congregations that have enjoyed success and that are admired by others as leaders in ministry, community listening can be a humbling process. People in the community may tell you things you don't want to hear. Some feedback you get may contradict your church's long-held assumptions about community needs and the best program models. The ministry model you have worked so hard to build may feel wobbly as people in the community ask you hard questions. All of this is worth it if it helps your congregation be more responsive to the community.

Reasons to Listen

So what are the reasons to listen to the community?

Listening Keeps Your Ministry Relevant

In order for churches to stay relevant to a changing world, we need to be very tuned in to what is happening "out there." One of the complaints about churches in the United States by nonchurchgoers is that the church "just isn't relevant to my daily life." How would it affect how you do ministry if you knew the following facts?

- Your neighborhood has one of the highest teen pregnancy rates in the nation.
- A majority of the people in your community are "un-churched"—have never attended church and don't now.
- There are many homebound, elderly people in the community who need friendly visitors and help with basic needs.
- If asked, many residents would be willing to volunteer in the community.

Knowing these things might influence what kinds of ministry programs you start, whom you ask to volunteer, and how you "do church" at your church. You may need to explore some less traditional worship models, such as meeting in a different location (perhaps the park?) and spending some Sunday mornings engaging in service projects together. Churches can get to an "inertia" point, where members are pretty comfortable with the way things are and don't want to change. Connecting with the people in your community can help pull you out of inertia and toward new ministry.

Being "on the ground" talking to people can also help make you aware of needs that you wouldn't hear about any other way. In my local community, for example, residents were talking about the foreclosure crisis long before the news hit the media. Nonprofits and churches that were paying attention to what residents were saying were able to develop responses on the front end of the crisis.

Listening Helps Identify Community Assets

Even if your church is located in a community that faces many challenges, you will find that the people and institutions there possess many "assets"—unique strengths, skills, passions, and abilities that help make the community a better place. Much has been written about the asset-based approach to community development, with *Building Communities from the Inside Out: A Path Toward Finding and Mobilizing a Community's Assets* by John P. Kretzmann and John L. McKnight (ACTA, 1993) as a seminal work on the topic. The Communities First Association and the Christian Community Development Association are groups that provide training and other resources on asset-based community development. These assets are what ought to undergird your community ministry efforts. One way to think about it—you are building on what is already good in your community, not just filling in potholes.

In my work I have run into many people who struggle in life, but they are still "asset-full." Standing at a distance, we may only see how a person or community struggles. But when we draw closer, we are more likely to notice the assets. A woman may be unemployed, but maybe her skill set isn't one that brings her a lot of money. She might sing, paint, or cook amazing dinners. A neighborhood may appear pretty rough at first glance, but once you spend some time there, you notice the beauty of the local park or the historic homes that have been lovingly restored. Community assets can be geographic or human, such as these:

- Great access to public transportation
- A beautiful park with a lake
- A farmers' market or community garden
- People who are active in their block club or neighborhood watch group
- A large number of artists who live in the area

Broadway United Methodist Church in Indianapolis has made a point of looking for assets in their neighborhood and then building on them. When the church was considering starting its own community garden, they decided to talk to the neighbors to assess interest level. They discovered forty-seven gardeners living within a few blocks of the church! So instead of starting their own garden, the church created opportunities for the gardeners who were already there.

Two young people from the neighborhood were hired to talk with the gardeners, asking them about what they grew, what they did with their produce, and whether they would be willing to sell it. Then associations and institutions in the community were asked whether they were interested in buying food from the gardeners. They were! The church was instrumental in getting a farmers' market started at the local hospital, with seed money from the hospital. Broadway pastor Mike Mather said, "Many of our gardeners plugged into the market. This was a way for them to make money and build relationships. They are doing a lot more than we could have accomplished if we had started our own garden!"

Listening Can Connect You to Potential Partners

Connecting with other organizations and people in your community can help you develop relationships that may be key to the implementation of your community ministry model. Groups you meet with could help you in a number of ways moving forward, including the following:

- Engaging with you in a program planning process
- Promoting your program and connecting your church with the people you wish to serve
- Providing use of a facility
- Sharing equipment and supplies
- Sharing staff time

Listening Can Help Engage Church Members

Sending congregation members out to listen can be a great way to engage them in developing new ministry. When they hear with their own ears and see with their own eyes the achievement gap in the schools, the homeless people on the street, or the unemployed workers seeking jobs, they may develop great passion. Your listening team may even become the core team for designing and implementing a new program.

Here are some listening dos and don'ts as you meet the neighbors:

- *Begin with a listening posture.* A listening posture is a deep desire to hear people, using listening as a way of expressing interest in others and great care and concern for them. This is different than connecting with others to plan, sell, solve problems, or close the deal.
- Do *listen more than you talk.* When meeting with someone new, it can be tempting to talk more, filling in silences with your own thoughts and ideas. Resist this urge and make listening your default mode.
- Do *express great interest in the person you are talking to.* Listening sessions are an opportunity to learn about the *people* you are talking to—their dreams, their backgrounds, their ideas and concerns. You are gathering information via a few specific questions, but be sure to take the opportunity to find out about the person too. How long have they lived in the neighborhood? What do they do for a living? What are their hobbies and interests?
- Do *take notes on the conversation, but ask for permission first.* Taking notes will enable you to refer back to capture the key ideas from the meeting. If you meet with the person

again (to pursue a partnership, for example), notes will help you remember what they said and build on it.

■ *Don't bring a preformulated plan to the meeting.* Too many people have complained to me, "They didn't really want to listen to me or hear my ideas—they had their plan figured out already." Many of the people you meet with may be suspicious that you don't really want to listen to them. By describing your solutions and plans during your meeting, you will confirm that assumption.

Ten Key Strategies for Meeting the Neighbors

1. Get to Know Community Members Who Attend Your Church.

The keys to getting to know your community may be very near, for the people in your own congregation who live or work in the community may be able to inform and direct your efforts. They are a great resource not to be ignored and the best place to start. If you aren't sure who these folks are, put out a call to the congregation for a meeting of church members who live or work in the community. Begin by asking these church members what they see as the top community needs and how they think your church could best respond.

People in your own church may give more open responses to your questions than the people you are meeting for the first time at other organizations. This is valuable! They may be able to tell you what has worked and what has failed in the community—including what your own congregation has tried in the past and how it turned out.

Engaging church members at this early stage in your process can also help to create "champions" for your work later on. Asking people for input can get them interested. They may be the first volunteers for your new community ministry efforts, and their enthusiasm will draw others.

Church members can also help you develop your contact list. Ask them which organizations and people would help you learn the most about your community, and see if your church members would be willing to connect you, perhaps even attending an interview with you. Sometimes I have made my way to "hidden" people in the community through church members—people who aren't real visible but who know a whole lot. Often they are longtime residents who have never held a formal title, but they know what youth do after school, which frail seniors stay in their homes, and how the local neighborhood association operates. Church members may also give you an "in" with someone prominent in the community who wouldn't be willing to see you without someone making the connection.

2. Meet One-on-One with Community Leaders.

Meeting one-on-one with community leaders is one of the best ways to learn about your community. Just keep in mind that "leaders" may not be the best contacts—such as the mayor, your city (or town) council member, or the pastor of the largest church in your area. These kinds of leaders may in fact be somewhat removed from what is happening on the ground in your community. You may get better insights and information from people such as community activists, school social workers, and engaged citizens who have been volunteering with organizations for years.

The kinds of people you will want to meet with will vary from community to community but may include the following:

NONPROFIT LEADERS

Look around your community for high-capacity nonprofit organizations—those with highly successful programs that make a significant impact in the community. Leaders of these organizations should be able to provide you with information on community needs, which approaches work best, and who is great to partner with (or not).

Look to these leaders as "experts" in the program areas in which they work. If you are looking for information on housing needs, the head of your local community development corporation should be able to help you. The director of a local day care center may know all about early childhood resources and which populations of children in your community do not have access to preschool.

Nonprofits may also be willing to share needs assessments they have conducted themselves, saving you the effort of trying to dig into a particular issue on your own. I recently received a needs assessment from a neighborhood nonprofit that focused on the educational needs of residents. This helped a church that I am working with identify that the community needs more GED (graduate equivalency diploma) resources.

CLERGY, STAFF, OR LAY LEADERS OF OTHER FAITH COMMUNITIES

Other faith communities may be able to help you learn. Look for congregations that have successful community ministry programs on the ground already. Their leaders can tell you what it took to get started, the bumps in the road along the way, and the keys to success.

In some congregations, the senior pastor or clergyperson is the best person to meet with; in others, you may want to connect with the ministry specialist that is most closely connected to the ministry area your church is interested in. If you have an interest in youth development, for example, you may want to meet with the youth pastor.

These meetings with other faith communities can also help sow the seeds for partnership down the road. Some of the best partnerships I have been involved with have started with like-minded people of faith sitting in a room together and talking about what is possible in the community.

COMMUNITY ACTIVISTS

Most communities have people whom I would call "community activists"—residents who are deeply engaged in community issues. They are frequent volunteers and may not hold a title or advanced degrees. They serve on the community council, head up neighborhood block clubs, volunteer at the community center, or work with youth on an informal basis, perhaps inviting kids into their own homes for tutoring or other activities. Older men and women who play a role like this are often seen as neighborhood "grandparents"—keeping an eye on the children and often everyone else too!

Community activists can tell you what is going on in the neighborhood day in and day out (and at night too!). Many have a historical sense of the community, how it has changed over the years, and how efforts at community improvement have turned out over the long-term. In my experience, they frequently have knowledge of developing community issues long before the media or formal organizations have knowledge of them.

To find community activists, you will have to do some networking beyond formal organizations in your community. Start by asking community residents in your church about connecting with the activists and then build your list of names. Once you start meeting with activists, ask them to refer you to other people who play a similar role in the community.

BUSINESS LEADERS

Don't forget about business leaders in your community. They will have a perspective that is different from the others on this list but just as valuable. Business leaders also care about what happens in the community, since community issues impact their future workforce, their ability to maintain a customer base, and the overall business climate. Here in the Twin Cities, a number of business leaders have become experts on and advocates for early childhood education, in part because they see the important link between school readiness and an educated workforce.

LAW ENFORCEMENT AND EMERGENCY PERSONNEL

Police, fire, and emergency personnel can, of course, tell you about crime in the community and other hard issues, but many also have a bird's-eye view of the services offered and which ones are needed. They are also interacting with families all the time on a variety of issues, so they can fill you in on topics such as levels of poverty and hunger, the condition of housing stock, and the status of new immigrant groups. Law enforcement may also have a sense of emerging community issues, witnessing trends or a direction a community is headed, for better or worse, before the news hits the papers (for example, movement of gangs or drug trafficking, or cultural or economic shifts in population).

SCHOOL PERSONNEL

People who work in your community schools can be a great source of information about the needs of children, youth, and their families. Starting with the school social worker is often the best bet. Social workers can inform you about unmet basic needs (food, clothing, shelter), who is struggling academically, and what kinds of support the families of schoolchildren need. A school social worker I met with recently talked about the children's need for jackets, snow pants, and boots; the number of children who go without food at the end of each month; and the high need for mental health services among the families served by the school. Information like this can aid your church in determining how you can help.

Other people to talk to at schools may include the principal, the assistant principal (often assigned to deal with students who struggle with behavior issues), and the school nurse, who can talk with you about health issues among students and the need for specific kinds of services. Lead teachers in certain academic areas (math, science, reading, arts) may be helpful if your church is looking into developing programs in one of those areas.

Schools and school districts often collect demographic data that may be available for public viewing. You might find that your schools collect demographic information that details race/ethnicity of students, where they live, how they are performing academically, and what percentage of students receive free or reduced lunches (an indicator of poverty). Sometimes this information is on the school or school district website, or you can ask staff how you might gain access to it.

3. Build Deeper Relationships with a Few Community Leaders.

Once you have conducted a few interviews, you may meet one or two community leaders whom you would like to get to know better. Think about the people you connected with most easily during your interviews and see if they might be willing to connect again, perhaps on a regular basis (monthly or quarterly). You might want to say something to them like, "I am working hard to learn more about our community, and you bring such a depth of experience and knowledge to your work. Would you be willing to meet with me occasionally to give me some advice and hear about what we are hoping to do?" Most people have a hard time saying no to that!

4. Hang Out Where the People in the Community Hang Out.

Every community has places where folks go just to hang out and spend time with each other. The kinds of places where this happens varies, based on your location (rural, urban, suburban) and the ethnic makeup of your community.

Social gathering places in your community might include the following:

- Coffee shop, diner, or other favorite restaurant
- Park or recreation center
- Fire station
- Barber shop or hair salon
- Beach, bike trail, or hiking path
- Local grocery or convenience store
- Sports fields or basketball courts

So what do you do when you arrive at the hang-out spot? You are there partly to observe—to see who lives in your community and what they like to talk about and do during their downtime. You may also learn something about demographics by just watching—are the people there old or young? Are there families with children? Are people dressed in such a way that you could gain clues about where they work (bus driver uniform, scrubs for medical personnel)?

Beyond just observing, you'll need to interact with folks as well, which may take some courage! I would recommend informal chats with people, rather than formal questioning (you will be seen as an interviewer if you carry a clipboard). I can tell you from personal experience that showing up at the same place repeatedly will help the people there develop a comfort level with you—they are likely to be more relaxed once they realize that you intend to stick around.

5. Attend Community Events.

Make a point to show up when the community gets together to celebrate or do some work. By showing up at these events, you are communicating that you care about the same things your neighbors do, that you are interested in building relationships and are willing to lend a hand. The kinds of events will vary from community to community but could include the following:

- Seasonal events (Memorial Day barbecue, Fourth of July parade, Christmas caroling)

- Community cleanup day, when neighbors pick up trash and plant flowers
- Celebrations hosted by particular cultural groups (Chinese New Year, Cinco de Mayo)
- Carnivals or other fund-raisers sponsored by other groups
- The annual meeting of your neighborhood association
- Crime prevention/block club events like National Night Out
- Summer festivals or community meals

6. Attend Community Groups That Convene Regularly.

Most communities have groups that convene regularly either to network or to come together to address a community issue (for example, the Chamber of Commerce, a ministerial alliance, or a human service council). Schools typically have parent-teacher or home-and-school organizations, a good place for your church to engage to learn more about the schoolchildren in your area (and to provide some much-needed help to the school).

Apart from being a place to learn about the community, groups like this can be a way to connect with potential partners—nonprofits, churches, government agencies, and businesses. When you sit at the table on a regular basis with people who are concerned about the same things as you, you might naturally begin to dream together about what is possible for your community and come up with some creative ideas for next steps. Plus, as you get to know the people around the table, you can get a more accurate sense about what they might be like to work with on a deeper level.

7. Volunteer in the Community.

You may eventually decide that mobilizing volunteers is your community ministry model of choice, but at the start, volunteering can also be a way to learn about the community. Send people out to work at the local food shelf, for example, and your church members will learn all about who is without food in your community (it may not be who you think). If your church members volunteer with an English as a second language (ESL) program, they will be face-to-face with newcomers from different ethnic traditions and perhaps who practice a different religion. They will learn all about the challenges that immigrants face to negotiate U.S. systems like public schools and health insurance.

Volunteering in community programs is a way to build relationships or partnerships with organizations in your community. Showing up to help is a great way to break the ice with groups you would like to find out more about and may lead to conversations about how you could work together.

8. Walk around the Community.

Walk around your community to get a totally different perspective. While walking around, you will notice things you wouldn't notice if you were in a car, such as:

- An up-close view of the condition of housing. Is paint peeling? Are roofs sagging? What homes are for sale, condemned, or being foreclosed? In what areas of the community is housing in particularly good condition—where residents have put a great deal of loving care into landscaping or fixing up older homes, for example?
- The ease (or difficulty) of getting certain places on foot. How easy or difficult is it for residents to get to your church if they don't have access to a car? What kinds of services are difficult for residents to access? If the only youth center in your community is on the other side of the freeway, for example, it may be difficult for the youth in your area to access it. Or maybe the grocery store is hard to get to on foot because it is at the top of a steep hill, or the local clinic is at the intersection of two very busy streets. Knowing this might lead your church toward a ministry of delivering groceries or transporting people to appointments.
- Where certain groups of people hang out. Where are youth? Where are mothers with small children? Where are senior citizens?
- Which local small businesses are located in your community. It is often hard to see small businesses from a moving car—such businesses often have small storefronts and minimal signage. Walking by gives you a chance to notice what kinds

of goods and services are sold in your community, as well as a chance to interact with business owners.

If you walk around regularly, people will begin to recognize you as a part of the fabric of the community. Especially in the city, people are often on the lookout for people who don't belong in the neighborhood (a crime prevention strategy). If you aren't someone they see often, they might be suspicious. But if you are always around, neighbors will begin to see you as a "regular," as someone who does belong. They may even begin to talk to you!

9. Go Door-to-Door in the Community.

This approach isn't for everyone, but your church might consider sending members out into the community to go door-to-door. First ask yourselves, "Would people in our community respond favorably to this approach? Is it safe for our church members to go out into the community?" If the answer to either question is "no," you'll want to stick with another of the strategies I have outlined here.

The value of this approach is that it may get you into contact with people who aren't connected to neighborhood institutions and who can't or won't attend community meetings. One church told me that their door-to-door canvassing helped them realize there were a number of homebound senior citizens in their community. Nobody knew about them because these seniors were unable to make it out to community meetings or even to the grocery store, in some cases. This knowledge helped the church change the focus of its community ministry vision.

If you decide to proceed with going door-to-door, I recommend that your canvassers always go out in pairs and focus on short, to-the-point conversations. Ask just two questions: "What are the key issues in this community?" and "What can our church do to help?"

This is not a time to promote your church—people often tell me that they want to use the door-to-door approach to give people a church brochure or video or invite them to a Sunday service. Resist the urge to do this. Just tell people that you want to know what they think and then thank them. It is better for your community ministry efforts overall if you don't give the impression that you are getting involved in the community just to recruit new church members. People expect church representatives who show up at their door to try to recruit them into something. Surprise them by just soliciting their opinions, thanking them, and then leaving.

10. Host a community event.

Consider hosting a community event at your church once you have completed some of the other meet-the-neighbors strategies. This could be a pancake breakfast, a barbecue, a game night, or a dessert/snack buffet. Events can help get group conversations started that wouldn't occur through some of the one-on-one strategies outlined here.

The people you talk to initially in your process can help you to promote your event and give you ideas for whom to invite. Always have food, and if you can't pull off a meal, just have dessert or snacks. Also, be sure to talk with people in the community about when to have the event—day of the week and time of day. Maybe many in your community have youth sports activities on Saturday mornings, for example, so hosting an event then just wouldn't work. In other communities, evening events may be problematic for young families or seniors who don't want to be out late or after dark.

Keep the "program" portion of the event simple—you just want people to meet the others at their table and have a conversation about community issues. Choose table hosts who can help people break the ice with each other and facilitate the conversation. Focus on just two or three questions, such as the following:

What are the key issues or needs in our community right now?
What are your dreams for our community—what do you hope happens here?
What other kinds of programs or initiatives are needed here?

Again, resist the urge to promote your church. You want to send the message that you are interested in your neighbors even if they would never come to church on a Sunday morning. This is truly a night for the community; see your church as playing a servant role to make it happen.

The Listening Never Stops

Meeting your neighbors and listening to them isn't just something that is important at the beginning of your journey toward starting new ministry. Meeting and listening ought to happen continuously even once you get your new ministry off the ground. Your first conversations may be the hardest, but as you get to know people, you will build trust with them and they will share more—their heartfelt hopes for their community and their deepest concerns. That first step of meeting the neighbors can lead you into deeper relationships with the people of your community.

Finding Your Congregation's Ministry Dream

What are your church members truly passionate about? What skills and gifts do they possess? And how does that translate into a ministry dream for your congregation?

Tapping into church members' passions can help you launch community ministry that has an exponentially greater impact than if just one or two staff members (or even church members) are trying to push an idea forward. Many successful congregations around the country have a "strong staff" model where staff do the research and design the programs then invite church members to volunteer (or maybe hire more staff to implement the program).

But I believe there is a better way. Strong direction from the pastor is essential, but pulling lay leaders in at the outset—empowering them to identify issues and inviting them to flesh out the ministry dream—leads to ministry with greater impact and staying power. In the end, your church members will also be equipped as leaders, bringing new skills for ministry into other areas of their lives.

Elements of a Ministry Dream

A ministry dream is more than a plan or list of tasks. It is a picture of all that your church could be in the community. It is often something that we can't achieve in our lifetimes. It is so big that it draws us into the future, into ministry efforts that we can't do without God. In fact, that is the first key element of a ministry dream.

- *Great ministry dreams push us toward God.* The dream is so big that we understand that we need God to give us wisdom we don't now have, to provide the resources and the courage we need.
- *Great ministry dreams push us toward each other.* To achieve the dream, we will need the gifts and talents of our fellow members. These dreams can't be realized by just a small handful of people. We will need to function as the body of Christ, unified in all its parts.
- *Great ministry dreams engage the community outside the church.* They are relevant to the community, recognizing what strengths and assets are already there, building on what has already been done.
- *Great ministry dreams focus on how people's lives will be changed.* Our dream should always ultimately be about the transformation of people, not just gathering money, starting programs, or building buildings.
- *Great ministry dreams are shared.* Though dreams may begin with one person (see "Where Does the Ministry Dream Come From?" below), the greatest dreams are those that are carried by many people, ideally the entire congregation.

Where Does the Ministry Dream Come From?

Ministry dreams begin in a variety of ways in the church. This process may vary depending on the culture of your church, your spiritual traditions, and the age and ethnicity of the people sitting in the pews. Here are a few places where ministry dreams could begin:

Your church history. Look into the history of your congregation to discover what kinds of connections to the community your church has had in the past. Sometimes a history of amazing service in the past can lead to another era of amazing service in the future. Church members may be inspired by the creativity and sacrifice of the past. Often congregations will have a "ministry theme" that runs throughout the congregation's history—a great emphasis on children and youth, for example. That focus may have been lived out in various ways over the years—an after-school program, a youth choir, a youth sports league—but somehow, it was always there.

Sometimes congregations are motivated by a negative history the church has with the community. Maybe the church mistreated the community or was unresponsive in a time of need. This may spur people on to a new era of service motivated by a desire to do things differently this time.

Your pastor. A visionary pastor may be the source of a ministry dream. Pastors with great gifts of discernment and preaching can see a picture of what the congregation is called to and then communicate it well to the people. Often this works best if there is a team of people to "catch the dream" after it is cast—to work out the details of developing a plan, engaging volunteers, raising money, and putting everything in place that is needed for the launch of a new ministry effort.

One church I served developed a tutoring program at a local public school because the pastor began preaching "off the page" one Sunday, calling out to people to begin to care about the public school three blocks away that happened to have the lowest test scores in the state. People heard that call and began to meet together about developing a tutoring program that eventually served a large number of students at two public schools in the neighborhood.

Prophetic voices. If prophetic gifts, such as knowledge, wisdom, and discernment are present and active in your church, it is possible that laypeople with these gifts will begin to step forward to encourage the congregation to move into new ministry. People may have a picture or a word from the Lord about how your church is to serve the community and may state it as a divine call to action. But sometimes these gifts are used more subtly, and you will have to pay close attention to what people are saying to you. In my own ministry life, I have noticed the prophetic at work when different people would come to me and say the same thing, sometimes the same words. God was trying to get my attention!

A formal process. You might choose to start an intentional visioning or planning process to surface the ministry dreams in your church. Such processes don't have to be prolonged or boring. You could invite intergenerational teams to dream big and draw pictures of their visions for the church, for example. I once facilitated an intergenerational process that involved people ages ten to eighty-five for a large Lutheran congregation. People in the same group were sharing about "what it's like to be a high school student today" and "what I was doing during World War II." It was a rich experience for everyone, and a vision for the congregation was created that took into account the many facets of that church's ministry.

Develop a visioning process that takes into account the "personality" of your congregation. If many of your members like to socialize, have house parties to dream together about what is possible. Churches with a more contemplative style may invite people to commit to a time of personal prayer and discernment and then call people together to share what they heard God say. If your congregation has an artistic bent, art can be woven into visioning processes in interesting ways. Ask people to write about their ministry dream in story, poetry, or song, or invite them to paint or draw an image of it.

Small groups. Small groups in your church that already meet together regularly for Bible study and fellowship could be a place where ministry dreams arise. This strategy uses a structure that already exists in your church to get conversations about community ministry started. Your church could even equip small group leaders with teaching tools on justice and community and see what people dream up. It is not unusual for members of a small group to form a nucleus of volunteers for a new ministry launch. If one of your goals is to motivate small groups into service, you may even set aside a part of each year to ask small groups to brainstorm about how they could serve, then ask group leaders to come together to share their ideas. Different small groups may come up with similar ideas—they could then combine into a larger group that could put more muscle behind a community ministry dream.

Like-minded church members. Church members who are passionate about a similar issue or type of ministry may come together and begin to dream. These kinds of groups often emerge organically when a few people get talking at coffee hour or in response to a sermon about social justice, for example. Maybe the people at your church who have a vision for developing an early childhood education center at your church get together to talk.

Community ministry planning team. Your ministry dream may arise out of your community ministry planning team, formed to begin to have conversations with leaders and organizations in the community. A lay leader or pastor might form such a team so that the church can be more strategic about engaging in the community, perhaps driven by a desire to better align ministries with the church's mission and strategic focus. In addition to connecting in the community, the team can also spend time talking to the people in your church about their interests and dreams. Forming a team like this is described below, using Elim Lutheran Church as an example. Your team gathers information through conversations in the community and congregation then recommends to the church some options for new ministry based on what they learned.

Partnering organizations with a dream. Your ministry dream may be developed in collaboration with one or more partner organizations that are outside your church, such as a local public school or housing nonprofit. Sometimes working with a like-minded group can give a better picture of what is possible. Partners might ask new questions, come with different ideas and resources, and may not be afraid to challenge the "sacred cows" within your church. I've found that dreaming with other organizations can cause a congregation to ask, "Why not?" and "Why can't we do it?"—good questions when you are looking at the best ways to serve the community.

Elim Lutheran Church Develops a Ministry Dream

Elim Lutheran Church is a congregation in Robbinsdale, Minnesota, a first-ring suburb of Minneapolis that has experienced dramatic demographic shifts in recent years. The church was founded in 1922 and was very connected to its community over the years, providing youth programming on-site in its gymnasium, and connecting volunteers to a local public school, among many other community initiatives. But in recent years, the congregation has been less involved in the community. The church is much smaller than it was, and many church members are elderly.

A new pastor decided that developing new community ministry opportunities was one of the keys to the church being able to move forward into a new era. Pastor Chris Enstad said, "Our church lies at a major crossroads (of two major streets) in the community, and our physical presence demands a physical response. Our community is right there—it's right outside our windows and doors." To get going, he invited a team of lay leaders to come to the table to discern how Elim might develop new community ministry. A diverse group of people formed the community ministry planning team.

The team spent several months meeting with a wide range of people in the community, asking these key questions:

- What are the key issues and needs here—in Robbinsdale or North Minneapolis (for example, lack of access to health care, seniors need support, youth need a place to go after school)?
- What other groups are working to address these needs and what are they doing? What kinds of partners does your group need to accomplish its work?
- What should our church do in the community that would be most helpful/needed?
- Is there anyone else we should be talking to about this?

Meetings were held with public officials, business owners, heads of nonprofit organizations, school leaders, clergy from other churches, and knowledgeable residents. Some of the team members had grown up in the community and still lived there, so they were able to connect other team members to potential interviewees. They also lent their historical perspective on the community to the process.

The group process helped the church focus on four possible community initiatives that were related to needs in the community as well as the interests of task force members: tutoring and mentoring of elementary-aged youth, teen programming, health programming (such as health checks and opportunities to exercise), and holistic support and care for seniors. A fifth possibility was added to the list because of the church's proximity to a new facility being built down the street: partnering with a new specialty care center for people with severe disabilities. After community interviews were completed, the group decided to ask the congregation about their interest in the five possible initiatives through coffee hour focus groups. A significant percentage of the congregation participated in the groups, which were facilitated by members of the community ministry planning team.

Here are the questions that were asked in the focus groups:

1. Based on our survey of the community, we have discovered that the following kinds of needs exist in Robbinsdale. Pick the one that is most interesting to you or that you would be most likely to engage with.

   A partnership or program that provides the following:
   □ Tutoring and mentoring for elementary school youth
   □ Community programming for teens and a place for them to hang out
   □ Preventive health programming: health checks plus opportunities to exercise and learn about healthy eating
   □ Spiritual and holistic support for senior citizens and their families, including caregiver support

2. Are there any other ways that you think Elim should be serving the community? What specific community needs do you see that Elim should be addressing?

3. Looking back at your time at Elim, how have you seen the congregation serve the community? What kinds of community ministry do you think Elim does best?

4. How do you use your gifts and skills currently at Elim? (We're looking for specific examples: teaching children, preparing meals, singing in the choir, etc.)

5. In what specific ways would you be willing to volunteer if Elim expands its community ministry programs?

Through the focus groups, church members expressed strong interest in Elim getting engaged in programming for children and youth. One of the groups interviewed in the Meet the Neighbors process was the nearby elementary school, and staff there had expressed a strong interest in partnering with Elim. Team members went back to the school to talk more specifically about how the church could provide volunteers and other resources.

By talking with the school social worker, principal, and staff from the school district, Elim members were able to identify the following opportunities to connect the church to the school:

- Sending in volunteers to tutor youth in reading and math (one-on-one, weekly)

- Forming a group of volunteers who would be willing to help with special events throughout the year. Help was needed for set-up and tear-down, seating people, and pouring coffee.
- Collecting items that students needed, particularly school supplies and winter gear. School staff requested snow pants in particular and suggested that church members donate gift cards from local stores so that families could purchase winter boots in the sizes needed.

At the time I am writing this, ten volunteers from Elim have been trained as tutors and have begun their work in the school. School supplies have been collected, and a winter gear drive is being planned. Volunteers have helped at special events, and there is discussion about how that could be done on an ongoing basis.

Clusters of Spiritual Gifts

Congregations can also have clusters of spiritual gifts, with more people possessing a particular spiritual gift than other gifts. These "clusters" can help give leaders insight into the types of ministries to pursue. Churches with a strong gift of teaching may mobilize volunteers out to teach English as a second language, tutor youth, and offer job training courses, for example. A strong mercy or healing gift might mean involvement in a health or counseling ministry.

If you're not sure which spiritual gift is strongest in your congregation, ask people to describe your church, particularly the impact it has had on their lives. You may hear familiar themes in those stories that will help you identify the predominant one or two spiritual gifts that are present in your church.

I recently completed a visioning process with a church that has a strong healing gift. People were asked to describe what the ministry of the church had meant to them, how they had grown and been changed by attending. Many people described healing as something they had experienced through their involvement in the congregation. Some people described physical healings—noticeable miracles that happened in an instant! Others described being healed in subtler ways—emotional wounds being healed because someone was willing to listen to them and not judge them, for example. Others talked about being healed of their harsh experiences in other churches where people attacked each other—at this church people were much more patient and respectful in their interactions. It was clear through what people said that healing was the primary spiritual gift present in the church.

This healing gift is apparent in a number of the church's ministries. A monthly healing service is held that is open to all. There is a "healing team" at the church who will pray with anyone who asks. And a number of people from the church have visited a mission partner in Haiti, with a particular focus on bringing needed medical resources.

You might also choose to use a written survey or inventory to help church members discover their spiritual gifts and ministry passions. I like the *LifeKeys* curriculum in particular (by Jane A. G. Kise, David Stark, and Sandra Krebs Hirsh, Bethany House, 2005). It covers spiritual gifts as well as personality types, passions, and values.

I think written surveys work best when combined with a class or sermon series on spiritual gifts, focusing on the key Scripture passages that describe the gifts and how they are to be used within the body of Christ. Don't make gifts inventories just another exercise in paperwork. They are an opportunity for people to begin talking together about how all gifts can be used in the church body and then to encourage each other in using their gifts. You might ask your network of Bible study or prayer groups to study spiritual gifts together and then help members identify how they will use their gifts in new ways—in the church and outside of it. Small groups can provide both accountability and encouragement in helping people use their gifts.

What Are Your People Passionate About?

So what are the people in your congregation passionate about and how can you tell? Are your people passionate about education and literacy? Access to health care? Making sure everyone has a safe and affordable place to live? Developing ministry out of the passions of the people will help ensure that the ministry will launch well and be sustainable into the future. Following are some tips on how to discern what your church members are most passionate about.

Observe where church members are working the hardest. Take a step back and look at where people in your church are most involved in volunteering at church. What volunteer opportunities does everyone sign up for? Maybe it is anything related to children and youth. And what kinds of work does nobody seem to want to do? Maybe in your case it is the fixer-upper tasks like cleaning, repairing, and painting. Pay attention to these choices as indicators of passions and interests.

Listen to what people are talking about. When you get into conversations with people at your church, what can they not stop talking about? Try to notice the patterns. Are you constantly getting into conversations at coffee hour about the large number of homeless people in your community or the state of the public schools? These might be indicators of where new ministry might begin.

Find out where people in your church are already engaged in your community. You might discover what people are most passionate about by looking at how church members are already engaged in the community through their volunteer involvement outside the church. If you have more Little League coaches at your church than you have ever seen in one place before, that is your clue that you have a large number of people interested in youth development (and in sports too!).

Ask church members through focus groups. Through focus groups, you can ask people directly what they are passionate about. Focus groups also afford the opportunity to get a large group of people involved all at once. You may get the greatest participation if you hold groups at a time when people are already at church (maybe during coffee hour?). I recommend groups of about eight people. Examples of focus group questions can be found earlier in this chapter in the story about Elim Lutheran.

Form a leadership team and dispatch them into the congregation to ask. You might decide to form a community ministry planning team early on. Part of the role of the team could be to go into the congregation to talk to people about what they are most passionate about. Team members could visit small groups, men's or women's gatherings, youth activities, or committee meetings to ask for community ministry thoughts and ideas.

Dreams Flourish in a Culture of "Yes"

To really fuel a culture of dreaming, it is important to establish a culture of "yes" in your church—a culture where people are encouraged to dream. In some congregations, there may have been a culture of "no" in the past, with staff and lay leaders discouraging conversation about what new work your congregation could do in the community. Sometimes concerns about finances fuel the "no" culture—how could we possibly take on anything new when we are struggling to meet our current financial obligations? Sometimes a culture of "no" comes from a fear of change. Really deciding to be more engaged in the community ought to involve change—in our priorities, in who is involved, and in what is important to us. But for people who see change as difficult, this will be a great challenge.

Be aware as you invite conversation about ministry dreams that it is important to move toward a culture of "yes" within your church. That is not to say that every dream that is brought forward will be developed into a plan and then implemented, but people need permission to think big and to dream. Encourage conversation and creativity and you may be surprised by how many people express interest in getting involved.

PART TWO

Models for Community Ministry

MODEL 1

Donate Goods or Money

WHAT IT IS: *Your church gathers donated goods (like school supplies or food) to donate to a community program. Or your church raises money for a specific purpose to benefit the community.*

Overflowing in a Wealth of Generosity

We want you to know, brothers and sisters, about the grace of God that has been granted to the churches of Macedonia; for during a severe ordeal of affliction, their abundant joy and their extreme poverty have overflowed in a wealth of generosity on their part. For as I can testify, they voluntarily gave according to their means, and even beyond their means, begging us earnestly for the privilege of sharing in this ministry to the saints.—2 CORINTHIANS 8:1-4

The church in Macedonia just could not stop giving. Paul says they "overflowed" in their generosity. This wasn't just a little trickle or a grudging donation of something left over that they didn't really want anyway. This was generosity that could not be stopped by adverse circumstances and the resulting discouragement. Even though the Macedonians had suffered a "severe ordeal of affliction" and were living in "extreme poverty," they were joyful and gave and gave and gave.

Oh, to be like the Macedonians, with generosity as a defining factor in our lives. To think first of giving, of our own needs much later. To give regardless of circumstances. To give with joy, not out of guilt. To be so bowled over by God and a desire to serve that we just cannot stop being generous.

Advantages of the Donation Model

This donation model is an easy place to start for churches that may be just beginning (or beginning again) to focus on community ministry. The model is relatively simple to implement, and I find that church members often enjoy the process of going out and purchasing items someone else can use. This seems to be an easier level of involvement for many people than volunteering. Donating doesn't require much of a time commitment, and your church members won't have to take the risks involved in personal interactions. One can be anonymous and give generously.

Another advantage is that this model can cost very little to implement, depending on the scale. (Very large collection projects that require warehouse space and vehicles would be an exception.) You may not have to hire staff to run this model, and you won't have the operational costs of running your own program on-site. A low-cost model may be easier to "sell" to church leaders if they are already feeling reticent about moving forward in community ministry or if members are nervous about adding anything to the church budget.

Another upside: donating can be a bridge to other more relational ministry models that are more complex and involve taking more risks. You can start here and use donating as a stepping-stone to a broader, more extensive community ministry strategy. Also, you can use the gathering of material goods as an opportunity to educate your congregation about the community issue you are focusing on. For example, if you are putting together toiletry kits for the local homeless shelter (to include toothbrush, toothpaste, deodorant, and soap), you can educate your congregation about who will be receiving them. Present facts about homelessness that your congregation may not be aware of—the percentage of the homeless who are women and children, veterans, or mentally ill, for example, or the fact that some homeless people have jobs but just can't make it financially on the wages paid by their employers.

Challenges of the Donation Model

A definite downside of Model 1 is that it can be much less relational than some of the other models profiled in this book. Sending needed items or money sure helps community efforts, but a greater benefit can occur if the people in your church and out in the community have the opportunity to get to know one another. In my experience, the fastest (and deepest) way to learn about your community is to sit eyeball to eyeball with someone from the community and hear his or her story. For example, you will learn a great deal more about what is happening in your local public school if you set foot in there every week and talk to teachers and students than if you simply back a truck up to the side door and unload school supplies. That said, donating money and supplies can be a first step toward developing relationships with the staff and clients of the organization you are supporting.

Another concern about this model is that it can lead to dependency for the people who receive the donated goods. (This depends on the kind of program you are partnering with.) For example, everyone needs food, but providing food may be just a Band-Aid for deeper issues that are causing the individuals and families in your community to need help getting food. For example, people may be out of work, struggling with illness or large medical bills, or battling addictions. So donating your food to a local food shelf isn't bad, but this alone may not help families move toward greater self-sufficiency because you aren't dealing with the underlying reasons they need food.

For that reason, I encounter more and more "basic-needs" non-profits that are beginning to ask what they can do to help families deal with deeper issues and move toward independence. If your church is supporting a local food shelf, you might ask the staff there how they are helping families get connected to resources to move out of poverty. I spoke to a food shelf director recently who said that she and her staff are beginning to talk to the families who come every month about their situations to try to understand if there is anything that can be done to help them move toward greater independence.

Also, if you think your church members will have a difficult time following directions on what to purchase, this could be a challenging model for your church to implement. If people just can't get it through their heads that you want *new* toys, not used ones, for example, or you are working with a charity that wants very particular types of items and your church members won't follow this list, your partner group or staff and volunteers at your church who have to sort through everything thoroughly to pull out the items that are not suitable may become frustrated.

This model may also be challenging for congregations with a significant number of unemployed members or members who are struggling financially. Your members may not have the financial resources to purchase items for someone else. They may be in a better position to donate their time as volunteers.

Always Ask about What Is Needed

I can't emphasize enough the importance of asking your partner what they need before collecting anything from your church members. What seems obvious to you as a needed item may not be, and receiving unwanted or unneeded donations can create a burden for your partner organization. Then staff members at your partner organization have to spend their precious time figuring out what to do with your donation, time that could have been spent doing important community work.

I once worked for a church that ran youth programs in the community. A partner organization dropped off a load of brand-new shoes one day. They were really nice shoes, but we had no place to store them, and we were not in the shoe distribution business. I had to spend time identifying another church or nonprofit that could use them. Those very nice shoes would have been a much better donation to a nearby program for the homeless that provided shoes as part of their programming.

I recently spoke to the director of a ministry that receives donated clothing and household goods. Their program has a specific list of items that they will and will not take—your partner may have a list like this too. This ministry loves to receive clothing, books, gift items, furniture, and children's toys. But please do not donate appliances, old electronics, and construction supplies or equipment. Her number one request: "Please do not donate anything that's broken, stained, or dirty!" (She frowned at me when she said it, remembering all of the old junk they have had to haul away.)

One way to make sure you get the items that are needed is to focus on one item at a time. One missions director told me about putting out a call for food shelf donations to her congregation. "Many people cleaned out their pantries and brought in really gross stuff—the strange food they received for Christmas that no one wanted to eat! These were not helpful donations for our partner food shelves!"

So the church changed its strategy for the next food drive. Their partners told them they really needed peanut butter and jelly. So the church asked members to bring peanut butter and "really good" jelly. Church members understood clearly what to buy and got excited and motivated when the jars of peanut butter and jelly were stacked into a huge pyramid in the church lobby. This church also does drives for a number of other specific items. For "Undie Sunday," hundreds of pairs of underwear were strung up on clotheslines in the church lobby. "It was over the top," the missions director told me, "but it worked. We must have collected over a thousand pairs of underwear. Plus this was an opportunity to educate our members that there are some people who are so poor that they cannot afford underwear."

Your partner may not want or need certain items for one or more of the following reasons:

- They already have an overabundance of that item. Some items are at the top of everyone's list to donate.
- They don't distribute that particular item as a part of their programming. Groups that provide housing may not distribute food; organizations that serve youth may not necessarily distribute school supplies. Ask to find out.
- Their customers can't use that particular item. I learned this anew recently when working on a school partnership. The women at the church I was working for were knitting mittens like crazy to give to community programs. But the social worker at the school said that *knitted* mittens were nearly useless for the schoolchildren. In our Minnesota winters, the mittens get wet and freeze, ensuring that the

children had cold, frozen hands when they came in from re-
cess. Not ideal! So she suggested that church members purchase nylon mittens to donate instead. We didn't know this
until we asked.

- They lack storage space or the right kind of storage space.
Your partner may not be able to store especially bulky items
or very large quantities of anything, so this is another thing
to ask about. Some items require a particular kind of storage
space—like a refrigerator or freezer, for example—and your
partner may not have that available. So ask.

Ask your partner about unusual items they need that nobody
else seems to want to provide. For example, everyone wants to
provide school supplies for kids, but how about school supplies
for teachers? Many teachers have to spend their own money on
classroom supplies each year. What if your church helped out with
that? You could purchase copy paper, art supplies, chalk, tissues,
hand sanitizer—teachers could give you a complete list of what they
need. Other less obvious items to purchase for a partner organization include new socks and underwear or feminine supplies for a
homeless shelter, a washing machine and dryer for use on-site at the
children's home, cleaning supplies and trash bags for the legal aid
office, a snow blower or fans and air conditioners for the local community center, and walkers or canes for an assisted living facility. Be
creative and start by asking your partner for ideas.

New or Used?

When gathering donated goods, the second most important question is to ask whether your partner wants new or used items. People
often make assumptions about this, and again, it can be frustrating
to have to sort through everything to identify what is usable and
what is not. If your partner accepts used items, do some teaching
with church members about what "good condition" means. Clothing that is stained or torn should be thrown away, not given to the
homeless shelter. I like to think about it like this: if it is not in good
enough condition for me or my family to use, it should probably be
thrown away.

A note about donating used computers, cell phones, and other technology: always ask before bringing over the four-year-old technology that you just replaced. I have known nonprofits that love to receive used computers so they can refurbish them to give away to community residents. I have known other groups that find them to be a burden—just something that needs to be hauled away. So call.

What Are Your Church Members Wired to Give?

Think about what your church members would be most likely to give based on their interests, stage of life, and networks. Congregations that are passionate about education may be interested in donating books. If health and fitness are a strong interest, your church may want to donate exercise equipment or healthy food. Outdoorsy types may want to give camp scholarships, funding for a trip to a local nature preserve, or hiking equipment.

Stage of life may also play a role in helping you determine what to donate. If you have a number of young families in your church, you may want to focus on items they are putting into their carts at the store on a regular basis—diapers, snacks for little kids, toys, infant items like car seats, pacifiers, bibs. Or if you have a number of seniors in your church who are moving out of their houses into apartments, they may have furniture or other household items to donate.

Suggestions for the Types of Items Your Church Could Donate

PERSONAL ITEMS
- Food, including ethnic foods preferred by new immigrants
- School supplies
- Underwear and socks
- Household items (pots and pans, bedding, towels)
- Feminine supplies
- Winter coats, hats, and mittens
- Sports equipment
- Clothing and shoes
- Toiletry kits—soap, shampoo, toothpaste, toothbrush

PROGRAM SUPPLIES
- Swimsuits and athletic gear
- Copy paper
- Electronic equipment like cameras, sound equipment
- Art supplies
- Furniture for offices or social areas
- New computers
- Party supplies
- Medical supplies

SPECIALTY ITEMS
- Washing machine and dryer
- Plants, trees, and shrubs for landscaping or a garden
- Tools
- Vehicles
- Sewing machines
- Industrial-sized refrigerator or freezer
- Building materials
- Gas cards or bus tokens

Crossroads Church Connects to New Immigrants

Crossroads Church, an Evangelical Covenant congregation in Woodbury, Minnesota, uses a hybrid community ministry model that includes gathering donated goods and money, mobilizing volunteers (see Model 2), and working with their partner organizations (see Model 3) in other ways. Lisa Adams, director of Missions and Care Ministries for the church, has worked to build close relationships with partner organizations so as to best understand what they really need. Before organizing drives for certain kinds of goods, she spends time with each organization to understand who their clients are, how they operate, what they need, and how goods are distributed. Forming relationships first has led the church to implement more targeted (and effective) drives for certain kinds of items.

One Crossroads project was to gather items for immigrants from Burma who had just arrived in the United States, working through a large, international nonprofit with a local affiliate. It was set up in a relational way—church members got to connect directly with immigrant families. One project tasked each small group in the church with purchasing a rice cooker and large bag of rice for one immigrant family. Each small group delivered the items to the home of one family. With an interpreter present to help everyone communicate with one another, church members were able to ask the family about their experience in a new country: "What's your story? Who's your family? What was the refugee camp like?"

Adams said, "Our people got to experience what it's like to live as a refugee, and that was critical. It was really stunning for a lot of our people to see that the families sleep on the floor. They need blankets but not fitted sheets! And a few of our people got connected to families as volunteers—helping read mail and transport people to appointments. You can talk about justice at a high level, but when you sit face-to-face with a new immigrant, you really learn about what life is like for them."

Recruiting volunteers to help with the items that are donated has been another critical element in the Crossroads program. Adams advises, "Always have a team of volunteers who are willing to take care of everything you collect. Sometimes our coat drives have gotten out of control! If you have ten carloads of coats, you really need a good team going. Ask your agency partners to come pick up the items on a particular day, and have a team of six to seven people who will help load everything up. That way your key volunteers get to meet staff from your partner organization, and the organization may ask your volunteers to come help when it's time to distribute the items."

Donating Money

Your church may decide to donate money instead of material goods. The good news—money is always needed! You may want to consider this option if your church members aren't excited about going shopping or if you have limited storage space at your church. I have also worked with partner organizations that much prefer to receive money so they can purchase the exact size, color, and type of items they need. It could be that your partners need items that would be difficult for the general public to purchase for them (curriculum, medical supplies, certain kinds of educational toys, etc.). And sometimes nonprofits can make bulk purchasing arrangements that would make your financial donations go much further than if every family in your church went to the store and bought one or two items.

Unrestricted Gifts

Your financial donation will be most useful to your partner organizations if it is unrestricted—that is, if it can be used for any expense within the organization: staff salaries and benefits, rent and utilities, whatever they need to spend money on to operate. In a time when unrestricted funding from foundation funders is becoming rarer and rarer, your congregation's leadership may decide simply to send the check without putting restrictions on how it can be spent.

Since many people like to give toward a specific purpose (see "Restricted Giving Packages"), if you want to support an organization in a less glamorous area (operational expenses) but know that totally unrestricted giving is a hard sell, you may be able to find creative ways to pitch such giving. First, ask your partner organizations about their greatest unfunded needs. Then get creative. One pastor suggested describing some less glamorous expenses like this: "The wheels on the bus keep the bus rolling!" campaign for vehicle maintenance or an "Apple a Day" campaign to highlight the importance of paying for staff health insurance (an entire wall covered with paper apples that church members "buy").

When most people give specific gifts like this, the unrestricted gift stands out as being particularly meaningful. If you choose the totally unrestricted giving option, it is important to communicate to the congregation the outcomes that will be achieved through the organizations you support. Develop compelling descriptions of the impact of the funding—program services offered, who is helped, and how they are able to move forward because your church members gave. It is that conversation about end results (see "Measuring Success in Your Ministry").

Restricted Giving Packages

While it is probably unrestricted funding that will be most useful to your partner organizations, I have found that most people like to donate to something specific—the more specific the better. Because our human nature wants to visualize exactly what our money is going toward, it is not unusual for donors to say to me, "I sent one kid to camp!" or "I am sponsoring one family in the transitional housing program." Knowing that one's check went toward the electric bill, gas for the van, or health insurance for staff just isn't as exciting.

Developing what I call "giving packages" for church members to donate to can be a great way to start a giving pattern in your church and new engagement with community ministry. The educational outcome here for church members is that giving packages help them to learn about what community organizations are doing and how their money can help. Maybe your partner is a local youth center and your giving packages focus on typical things like camp scholarships and the tutoring program. But your partner may also run a cooking program to help youth learn about preparing meals—and through the program, supper is provided to kids who may not have much to eat at home. Including a program like that in your giving list will help to educate church members about the situations youth in your community face.

Talk to your partner organization about what they need funding for, and be creative about figuring out how much each of these items would cost. You could ask everyone to give to one big item (like purchasing a bus) or offer a list of options, from small to large. Avoid the temptation to leave larger items off the list because you don't think anyone will give to them. You might be surprised by the responses you get. I once included a $2,400 category on a mailing I sent out (sponsor one student in the tutoring program for an entire year!), thinking no one would take me up on that giving package. But we received a check for $2,400 in the mail from a church member whom I never would have expected to respond to a request that large.

Some "Giving Package" Options:

- Camp scholarships—send one kid to camp
- Underwrite the cost of an entire program
- Sponsor a community event
- Underwrite a new staff position—a youth director at the rec center or a case manager at the shelter-in-place agency
- Purchase a truck, van, or bus
- Cover a specific number of program sessions—six ESL classes, three job training sessions
- Sponsor staff or volunteer training
- Cover the cost of a certain number of meals at a shelter
- Pay for one plot in the community garden (materials, water, staff cost of running the garden program)
- Pay for the cost of a guest artist for the arts program
- Underwrite the operation of one housing unit in your affordable housing program
- Cover the cost of one medical checkup
- Pay for one computer for the computer lab
- Sponsor a local sports team (uniforms, athletic equipment, staff time, gym time, snacks)

Making Generosity a Habit

The best outcome for your congregation in setting up a giving campaign or program is that generosity becomes a habit. We shouldn't just think about giving once or twice a year when we are asked to donate a turkey or give to the camp scholarship drive. It ought to go deeper than that. Starting giving patterns in churches can be transformative for members all year-round, when we reorient ourselves toward thinking about how we can share all that we have even when no one asks us to.

Getting started on giving this way can also lead to a spirit of generosity for your congregation in other areas. Congregations that aren't used to thinking about the needs of the surrounding community and how they might help might start "getting the hang" of that through this model. Learning to give is the key to implementing any of the models in this book. Starting here could lead your congregation into much more extensive community ministry in the future.

What You'll Need

- One or more partner organizations to receive your organization's donations
- Information on what the organization needs—the more specific the better
- Some ideas about what your congregation is likely to donate—know your congregation well
- Ways to communicate to your congregation about what they can give
- A place for people to drop off their donations
- A place to store donations if your partner can't accept them right away
- A way to transport donated goods to your partner

MODEL 2

Mobilize Volunteers

WHAT IT IS: *Sending church members out into the community to volunteer for programs and organizations outside your church. Mobilizing volunteers is one key component (among several) of Model 3: "Partner with Other Organizations."*

We Were Made to Serve

"Whoever wishes to become great among you must be your servant, and whoever wishes to be first among you must be slave of all. For the Son of Man came not to be served but to serve, and to give his life a ransom for many."—MARK 10:43-45

God made us to serve—that's the truth. God gave us unique gifts and callings—that's the truth. As Christians, we are to express care and concern for our fellow community members—that's the truth. Focusing on these truths is the best way to mobilize volunteers out into the community.

There are certainly other ways to convince volunteers to serve. Using guilt might work—for a while. But it gives your whole effort a negative flavor. And serving in the community isn't just about getting work done. Mobilizing church members by giving them a checklist of tasks or projects to complete might mean that when those are completed, your volunteer effort loses steam. God's way is better. He calls us to make serving others a way of life. If congregations take up this teaching, helping to ingrain the truth and promote lifestyle changes that make room for service, no organization in this country should be hurting for volunteers. Pastors will have to encourage believers from the pulpit to set new life priorities, to set their schedules before God and ask the Holy Spirit to show them what needs to go. Christian education will need to focus on godly uses of time and talent. And youth and children's programs will need to include service components.

The best outcome for this model is that your church members develop a lifelong habit of volunteering, not just that you send a hundred volunteers into the local public schools. You are asking people to make space in their lives for service—a tall order for many. For some of your members, it may mean cutting out something else that matters a great deal to them.

The Upside of Mobilizing Volunteers

One of the advantages of this volunteer model is that your church will be connecting with efforts that are already taking place in the community. You don't have to start from scratch and assess needs and develop programs and infrastructure. You can just look for existing well-run programs and see how volunteers from your congregation might help. For example, the homeless shelter in your area may have a need for volunteers to help with the following tasks:

- Serving meals
- Providing job coaching to residents
- Running a tutoring program for the children who live at the shelter
- Being a chaperone for recreational events for residents (going to a sporting event, for example)
- Serving on the board of directors
- Helping plan and staff the annual fund-raising banquet
- Sewing blankets to be used by residents
- Painting and cleaning the facility

By plugging into what is already happening in the community, you avoid duplicating effort. Your resources won't be funneled into creating a program just like something that already exists, but into building a program that is already good into something better. Think of volunteers from your church as the missing puzzle piece needed by many of the organizations in your community.

Volunteering is a two-way street—an opportunity for your church members to receive as much as they are giving. We *are* called to serve, but I have experienced (and heard from many other volunteers) that what we receive from volunteering is more significant than what we give. Volunteers receive new knowledge, develop a new understanding of life in the community, and form new relationships. Volunteers also learn how to make room in their lives for service, reordering priorities in life in order to give.

This model can be a good fit for churches that have limited capacity to start and manage their own programs, such as starting a church-run homeless shelter on-site. Perhaps administration and management are not your congregation's giftings, making models 6 and 7 in this book (developing a ministry program or a church-based nonprofit) nearly impossible to begin and sustain. Or your capacity may be limited by your relatively small group of church members. Partnering by sending volunteers can get more people into the front lines of ministry, taking people out of the job of building the infrastructure required for a new program or organization.

Another advantage of the volunteer model is that an effort to mobilize volunteers can also be much more relational than a number of the other community ministry models (though not all volunteer opportunities are relational—see pages 56–60 in this chapter). Relational ministry is best, as I reiterate a number of times in this book, because it brings about the greatest change in the community and in your church. Being face-to-face with each other is transformative. We learn about the challenges other people face and the gifts they possess. In my experience, relational ministry does more than anything else to break down barriers between people. It is harder to make generalizations about poor people, suburbanites, immigrants, white women, or _____ (you fill in the blank) when you are developing a relationship with someone in that group who defies the stereotypes.

Challenges and Disadvantages of the Volunteer Model

One downside of the volunteer model is that it limits you to working with existing efforts in your community. You may not be able to find an organization that is willing or able to take volunteers from your church. I have sometimes worked in communities with fairly low-capacity nonprofits that aren't used to using volunteers or aren't equipped to receive them. Or you may find it difficult to identify a partner that matches/complements the particular interests of your congregation. For example, if your church members are wired to work with children and youth and the average age of residents in your community is sixty-seven, finding an organization nearby that fits may be challenging. Or maybe you have a church full of artists in a community that is dominated by sports.

Focusing on sending volunteers also will likely take you out of the creative process of designing new ministry efforts that meet unique community needs. For congregations that are bursting with creative energy to create new programs and ministries, using the volunteer model will be hard (and may mean that Model 2 isn't for you). Also, it is possible that sticking with mobilizing volunteers will cause at least some church members to feel less ownership for community ministry efforts. People may be more likely to think of a ministry as "theirs" if it is operating just down the hall from the sanctuary or one floor up.

Another challenge can be the amount of time your church members have (or don't have) to volunteer. Some congregations are filled with people who move at a breakneck pace through life, with high demands on the job and a busy home life filled with ferrying children to soccer games and music lessons. Throw in other issues like taking care of aging parents and there may be some people in your congregation who really don't have time to volunteer.

One way to respond to this challenge is to ask church members which kinds of opportunities they would be most likely to say yes to. Time-crunched people may be more likely to volunteer through something they are already participating in at church, such as their small group or the women's ministry. Families may be more likely to engage if parents can volunteer with their children, creating an opportunity to serve and spend time together.

Do Church Members Have to Volunteer through Your Church?

Church leaders often ask me if church members need to volunteer through the congregation or if outside volunteer opportunities they have arranged themselves "count" (e.g., coaching a local Little League team or serving on the PTA). The answer of course is that yes, they count. I encountered several churches in the process of writing this book whose leaders found that many members were already plugged into community activities as volunteers, serving as Cub Scout den mothers and fathers, board members of nonprofits, tutors, mentors, volunteer construction workers—and the list goes on. These congregations decided that those commitments needed to "count" when the congregation was assessing how the church was connected to the community. One congregation chose not to start anything new but to simply encourage members to keep up the good work, highlighting in the Sunday service some of the organizations where they were already involved.

As you decide how and whether to create new volunteer opportunities, keep current involvements of your members in view. If you decide that a much larger percentage of your congregation ought to be volunteering somewhere, keep your already engaged members in the loop by inviting them to share about the joys of volunteering and to encourage other members to get out and serve. You could also invite members who volunteer to help develop opportunities at the organizations where they serve so that more volunteers from your church could serve with them there.

From One-Time Events to Consistent Volunteering

A large congregation in the outer suburbs of the Twin Cities has made volunteering a centerpiece of its youth ministry. Over 350 people from the church, including youth and their mentors, volunteer once a month at more than thirty sites in the community. The church used to focus on large, one-time events, sending volunteers out to a one-day community carnival, for example. A former pastor at the church said such events were just too time-consuming. "So many people had to put in so much time, and it took up quite a bit of our budget too. There was no lead-up to the event, nothing that happened after, and no reflection time for our volunteers. We started asking ourselves, 'Why are we doing this?'" Instead, the church developed four "service environments": Serve Your Community (local opportunities), Serve the City, Serve a Meal, Know and Be Known (relational opportunities). The groups selected now include several shelters for the homeless, the local food shelf, facilities for adults with disabilities, and senior living complexes. Volunteers can participate in hands-on tasks, like sorting clothes, or relational opportunities, like visiting with a resident of a senior center. The church has also made a way for people with needs in their own congregation to benefit. Volunteers go to the homes of church members to help out people with health issues or who have experienced a traumatic event such as a death in the family.

What has been the secret to the success of the effort? The pastor says that volunteers need to be "both excited and equipped." She adds, "People need to see the vision for this and understand the 'why'—it's because you and I need to change and grow, and the flip side is that there's a world of people in pain out there whom we can be with and come alongside."

Three Types of Volunteers

There are basically three types of volunteers, based on the type of work church members tend to do or be drawn toward. Each type of volunteer will fill a different role in your volunteer program, allowing you to involve a variety of people in the work. It is important to note that one individual may have skills that fall into several categories, but because of other factors—age, stage of life, health issues, and work and family schedules—they may need to stick with volunteer opportunities in just one of the categories.

The introvert-extrovert difference may also play a role in which types of opportunities church members select for themselves. Introverts may like to work on projects by themselves, even choosing ones they can work on in the privacy of their own homes, and may shy away from group opportunities. Extroverts may prefer to work on projects in groups and gravitate toward opportunities that involve face time with people.

Hands-on volunteers are people who literally put their hands on what needs to get done for good ministry to happen. They build things or fix things, they go and get supplies, and they set up or break down a space for ministry. Hands-on volunteers are there on the annual cleanup day at church cleaning in all the corners, painting, and hauling the junk out of the church and to the dump! These kinds of volunteer opportunities may be shorter-term—ideal for people who can't commit to showing up for a weekly commitment like tutoring children but who can gear up for an occasional project.

My dad was a hands-on volunteer in his own church. Dad fixed the church buses, rebuilt and painted the church sign, bailed water out of the basement and cleaned up the mess, fixed the roofs of the church and parsonage, planted flowers in the front, and installed hand railings in the church. And he did all that in a matter of about three months! He blessed the people of his church and community by using his hands.

Leadership volunteers are good at helping groups of people develop vision and then leading them toward the goal. They tend to be big-picture thinkers and good communicators and have great trouble-shooting skills. The committees they run at church go far— they are good at helping groups set goals, develop plans, and hold well-organized meetings.

The work of leadership volunteers often results in expanded institutional capacity for any group they are working with. The work they do could raise the ability of the organization to plan, hire personnel, or design programs. This type of volunteer is also good at developing processes and policies—working on your personnel policy manual, for example, or designing a process for recruiting and training volunteers. In addition to helping build capacity in your church, they might be sent out to partner organizations as board members or strategic planners.

Relational volunteers are the teachers and mentors in your congregation. They are people who sign up for face-to-face volunteer opportunities because they love nothing more than seeing people develop themselves and become who God means for them to be. They have great insight into the potential and giftedness of people and often have the patience required to walk with individuals or groups of people over a period of time while they are learning and developing. This type of volunteer may also have a creative bent and the ability to design programs well.

In my own childhood, I was fortunate enough to have volunteers like this working with me as my Sunday school teachers. They had a passion for children and endless creativity in designing activities, including Bible memorization contests, Christmas pageants, puppet shows, plays, and dramas. They created an almost magical atmosphere for me at church, and I wanted to go every Sunday. I am still reaping the benefits of knowing them.

Relational volunteers make (and experience) the greatest impact if they are involved consistently and over the long term. By relating to someone regularly (perhaps weekly or even more often), barriers fall down, trust is built, and change can be experienced by both the volunteer and the person he or she is in relationship with.

Sample Volunteer Tasks/Activities for the Three Types of Volunteers

HANDS-ON VOLUNTEERS	LEADERSHIP VOLUNTEERS	RELATIONAL VOLUNTEERS
• Remodel a classroom	• Serve on a board of directors	• Tutor someone
• Fix the plumbing	• Facilitate a planning process	• Mentor someone
• Install and maintain a garden	• Plan a fund-raising event	• Provide job coaching or training
• Cut and assemble materials for a craft project	• Build a collaborative relationship with another organization	• Teach an ESL class
• Sew blankets		• Teach a GED class
• Pack up an organization that is moving then unpack them	• Provide financial advice to an organization	• Teach a personal financial management class
• Stock shelves	• Convene an advisory group for a program	• Lead an arts activity
• Pick up something with your vehicle and drop it off	• Conduct focus groups to evaluate a program	• Coach a sports team
• Clean the floor		• Read to children
• Paint walls	• Recruit and train volunteers	• Provide medical checks
• Prepare a meal	• Develop policies and procedures for an organization	• Lead an exercise class or walking group
• Fix or install computers		• Work in the garden with residents
• Fix and maintain vehicles	• Develop a budget	
• Go shopping and buy supplies	• Write a grant proposal	• Form a neighborhood watch
• Set up for an event then clean up afterward	• Write a newsletter	• Talk about your career to a group of youth
• Transport participants	• Create a website	• Lead a support group

Choose a Partner

One of the most important aspects of the Mobilize Volunteers model is choosing the right partner. You are looking for volunteer opportunities for your church members that would be meaningful for them and that fit their passions, interests, and skills. You are also looking to bless your partner, sending volunteers to do work that actually needs to be done. Will you mobilize your volunteers to the local public school, a nearby park, a senior center, or the community garden? Model 3: "Partner with Other Organizations" outlines steps to take to ensure that you end up with the right partner.

Recruiting Volunteers

Create Opportunities

Most people want to help, but they want to know exactly what it is you need them to do. It is hard to say yes to a vague job description such as "Just show up and help us with our youth club." People fear being asked to do something that makes them uncomfortable.

Developing volunteer job descriptions will also help your church members to understand whether this opportunity is something they are passionate about—or not. Then you can avoid the situation where people say yes quickly without understanding what the job is going to entail. That kind of mismatch can lead volunteers to give up shortly after they have started—a situation you want to avoid.

Your partner group may have already developed specific volunteer opportunities—if so, you may be able to use their materials to communicate opportunities to the congregation. If your partner group has not already done this, work with them to break volunteer opportunities into many different bite-sized opportunities, identifying the specific tasks volunteers will be involved in completing, how often they need to come, and the overall time commitment. You want people to look at these opportunities and say, "Yes, I could do that!"

For example, for your partnership with a local preschool, you might break volunteering into the following "bite-sized" opportunities:

- Read books to children one hour per week.
- Lead group games in the gym on Tuesdays and Thursdays for one hour.
- Prepare and serve a snack on-site once a week.
- Work with students on completing a craft project twice just before Christmas.

- Paint the classrooms and plant the garden on a twice-a-year project day.
- Teach science curriculum that includes hands-on science experiments every Wednesday for two hours.
- Help chaperone field trips as they occur—usually six times per year.
- Serve on the advisory council for the center, helping to develop policies and raise money.

Sample Volunteer Job Description

Develop a job description, even if it is brief, for each volunteer opportunity you are recruiting church members to sign up for. Job descriptions should include the following:

- The title of the volunteer job
- Location of the volunteer opportunity
- Key tasks the volunteer will be expected to complete
- The timing and frequency of the volunteer opportunity (for example, every Tuesday evening during the school year from 7:00 to 9:00 p.m.)
- Amount of time required to serve weekly or monthly
- Any preparation or training the volunteer will be expected to complete
- The person the volunteer will be reporting to

Different Ages and Stages

Volunteer opportunities ought to be matched to the age and life stage of the people in your congregation. Consider what clusters of age groups you have—lots of "young" seniors (ages sixty to seventy-five), a boatload of teenagers, or baby boomers galore. Then think about life stage. Young families tend to be the most pressed for time, as parents juggle their own obligations as well as their children's. New retirees may be looking for volunteer opportunities during the day. Young singles may be interested in serving with other people in their age/stage group as a way to build community.

Families in your church may be interested in volunteering with their children, so look for organizations that allow children to serve. Serving a meal together or doing neighborhood cleanup are two good options for families. My family helped with a neighborhood cleanup when our daughter was a year old. She was carried in a backpack on my husband's back! Our son, who was five at the time, took great joy in picking up trash.

Keep in mind that aging seniors may have health limitations that would make it difficult to do certain kinds of work—something that involves a lot of walking or heavy lifting, for example. That said, I recently met a couple of seniors who are over eighty-five, who said they have had to "cut back" their volunteering to "just" three days a week. They also both serve on a couple of boards!

Communicate Opportunities

To get people to engage in volunteering, you will need to tell them, and tell them, and tell them about the opportunities, and then tell them some more! Communicating often and through a variety of media will help ensure the success of Model 2 in your church.

Pulpit Time

There is no substitute for pulpit time when it comes to encouraging church members to move on something. We are all sitting right there in our seats, ready to be talked to! Plus, having your pastor endorse your efforts will encourage church members to participate. *Sermons* on serving the community can promote a spiritual conversation within the church, encouraging your members to see service as a key part of their faith, not just another obligation or item on their check-off list.

Testimonials and announcements from the pulpit are also highly effective. Ask lay leaders who can give compelling *short* testimonies or announcements to speak. There is no substitute for engaged volunteers who can describe their love for and interest in the work and their joy at seeing change happen—in themselves and in the community.

Other Opportunities

Guest speakers. Invite people from the organization where you are serving to speak. Hearing about the work firsthand from someone on the front lines may inspire your members to serve.

Church newsletter. Use articles in your church newsletter to highlight the work of your partner organizations and to feature the stories of individual volunteers from your church. What are they learning, what impact are they making?

Church bulletin. Short blurbs highlighting the volunteer opportunities work best in church bulletins. Include what the opportunity is, when it occurs, where it is at, and how to sign up. Think about including ongoing volunteer opportunities in the weekly calendar listed in the bulletin—this communicates that volunteering is a regular part of church life, just off-site.

Church website or email updates. Keep stories about your community ministry efforts in front of people via the church website and email updates. Keep them short and include lots of photos.

Small groups and committees. Use existing groups at your church to spread the word about volunteer opportunities. Some groups may even want to volunteer together as a part of their time as a group.

Social media. Post volunteer opportunities on Facebook and get a Twitter feed going to attract new volunteers.

Word of mouth. In some congregations, word of mouth works better than any other form of communication. In one church I served, the choir members were the communication hub for the whole church. If you wanted news spread fast (good or bad), there were about five choir members who would get the job done right now! We spread the word about the good work of our tutoring program through choir members. Soon the whole church was buzzing about our wonderful program, and many more volunteers signed up as a result.

Training Volunteers

Your volunteers will need to receive training before they start, and the content of that will vary depending on the roles your volunteers will be playing and the type of organization you are partnered with. It is ideal if your partner organization can provide the training or at least a part of it. If training volunteers is something your church does well, you may be able to work with your partner to develop the training. In a few cases, I have worked with very small nonprofits that are not in a position to provide training for volunteers. In this case, your church might try to do it, or you might be able to find another partner nonprofit with this competency that would be willing to help out.

Training could be structured and formal or more informal in nature and could cover topics such as the following:

- Expectations of volunteers—length of commitment, nature of commitment, job duties, support available to volunteers
- Training in the curriculum or method the volunteers will be expected to use. If working as a tutor, you might be trained in the reading curriculum; as a caseworker for the homeless, you would receive training on interviewing techniques and how to keep case notes.
- Safety concerns and procedures, including sexual abuse prevention/safe child policies, physical safety, safe use of the building and equipment
- Mandatory reporting requirements for suspected child abuse and neglect
- Appropriate relationships and boundaries
- Ethical or legal issues or concerns, including the importance of confidentiality
- Special procedures to ensure the safety of particularly vulnerable populations, such as people with disabilities or frail seniors
- Strategies for working in a multicultural/multiethnic context
- Process for addressing concerns—volunteer's concerns or those of others

Background Checks

If your volunteers will be working directly with children or vulnerable adults, you will want to conduct criminal background checks of those volunteers. Volunteers who will be driving as part of their duties should also have their driving records checked and insurance coverage confirmed. These checks can now be done easily online. Numerous companies provide this service for a fee. Check to see if your denomination has a membership with one of the services (which may lower your cost) or if denominational staff have recommendations on which service to use.

Celebrate Your Volunteers

Don't forget to thank your volunteers on a regular basis. People appreciate being told "Thank you!" verbally or in writing and usually don't expect some fancy prize or reward. You might consider holding an annual appreciation event for your volunteers—a dinner or coffee time, for example. And be sure to include a thank-you for volunteers during all-church events held during the year. This keeps your community ministry efforts in front of the congregation and allows you to remind people who aren't currently volunteering that they could! Highlighting the work of one or two outstanding volunteers may be helpful, calling your other volunteers toward even greater excellence and capturing the imagination of the congregation about what is possible. Always include a way for new volunteers to sign up—place sign up cards on each table, for example, or a staffed display somewhere in the room where people can get information about volunteering and sign up.

What You'll Need

- A core group of church members who are excited about going into the community to volunteer
- Partner organizations that do work in an area that your members are excited about and that can provide a good experience for your volunteers
- Specific volunteer opportunities and written job descriptions for those opportunities
- Ways to promote volunteer opportunities
- People who will follow up with volunteers once they have signed up
- A way to train your volunteers

MODEL 3

Partner with Other Organizations

WHAT IT IS: *A more full-fledged partnership with a nonprofit, church, or other organization that involves mobilizing volunteers but also other kinds of connections, such as contributing funds, helping with events, coplanning programs, and potentially even sharing staff, facilities and fund-raising together.*

Find Your Missing Piece

Indeed, the body does not consist of one member, but of many. . . . If the whole body were an eye, where would the hearing be? If the whole body were hearing, where would the sense of smell be? But as it is, God arranged the members in the body, each one of them, as he chose.—1 CORINTHIANS 12:14,17-18

God made us so that we can't do everything ourselves. We need each other. The best ministry acknowledges this at the outset; that is part of what makes the partnership model so powerful. You say at the beginning, we are in need of others to make this happen, with their gifts, passions, and abilities that balance and complement ours. You approach others seeking their giftedness and acknowledging their importance.

In ministry we need artists and inventors as well as administrators and planners. Introverts balance extroverts. When it comes to spiritual gifts, teachers, preachers, healers, helpers, and encouragers all come together and make a whole that is much greater than those parts. Pursuing partnership is an acknowledgment that we need other people to move forward on our own visions. We are all part of the body, serving God's people in the world.

The Advantages of Partnering

One of the greatest reasons to partner is the synergy that can develop when different people and organizations that are passionate about a cause come together. Some church leaders have described this to me as "not duplicating what is already occurring in our community." But I think the idea behind partnering is greater than that. When partnership is done well, the result is often many times greater than what an individual organization can do by itself. Often it is because a larger group of people bring more ideas, gifts, and skills. Also, partnerships create a greater opportunity for testing, trying, and challenging ideas—if the people involved are willing to be honest with one another.

One of my pastor friends described to me how his large suburban church began a partnership with a small urban church. He said the urban pastor called him and said, "Why don't you come down and see what we're doing, and maybe your half and our half can come together and make a whole." The very best partnerships are like this—your partner is the missing piece! What they bring just fits.

Partnering can also be a great model for your church if you can't or don't want to put the time and energy required into building a program or nonprofit or if you lack the capacity to develop a "home-grown" program or organization. Depending on how you structure this model, your partner may well be the one that takes on many of the administrative and programmatic tasks. They create volunteer opportunities (perhaps with your advice), train the volunteers, and provide supervision for them on-site. Your partner may also host the program at their site and handle things like budgeting, financial reports, staff supervision, and property management—a real boon to your congregation if you lack these administrative capacities or are too small to devote staff time to these areas.

Partnering can also be a way to maximize limited resources. You may bring a wealth of some things to the table and a shortage of others. This model can be a great fit for the small church, in particular, where staff time and financial resources may already be stretched to the limit. Your partner can help fill in the gaps in the areas where your church is running short. Following are some examples:

- You have a lot of space in your facility but a shortage of staff time to offer to the community. Your partner supplies the people.
- You have many volunteers but no funding for needed supplies or equipment. Your partner is a well-financed nonprofit that just needs volunteers.
- You have money and strong interest in the congregation in making in-kind donations, but you lack the expertise to launch and manage a program. You partner with an existing program in the community.

Challenges of Partnering

Partnering takes more work than some of the other models here, plain and simple. When I asked a friend whom I consider to be the "queen of collaboration" what she would say to congregations wanting to partner, she thought for a good long while and then said, "It's hard!" Partnering is hard because you have to take the time to sort out the roles of the different partners—who is doing what, when, and where, and who is paying for it. Usually you need to keep having this conversation during the course of the partnership, reinforcing and clarifying what you initially decided.

Also, partnering takes more time than some of the other models outlined here—depending on how your partnership is structured, it could take considerably more time. Ongoing meetings with your partners about details of the partnership take time. Coordinating schedules between two or more organizations adds a layer of complexity that isn't present in some of the other models—program schedules, staff meeting schedules, community meeting schedules, and so on. If you are fund-raising together, for example, plan to double or triple the amount of time spent working on grant proposals to get all of the information from everyone and to get the needed approvals.

And partnerships almost always involve compromise. Everything may not be exactly the way your church wants it. You may need to "give" in a number of areas, including the content of programs, the size of the budget, and the roles of staff. If your church is truly an "entrepreneurial" church, creating and launching its own programs with its own distinctive mark, then the partnership model may not be for you.

And keep in mind that sometimes partnerships just don't work. One missions pastor at a large church told me that he thought only about 40 percent of their partnerships end up working well in the end. "We like to invest in great people who have a neat idea, but they don't always have the capacity to make the idea a reality. One group talked well about what they wanted to do, but it was hard for them to translate that into community transformation. Another partner never got to the point of financial transparency; the financial reports just didn't look right."

He noted that most churches are not willing to partner with groups that fail, and that it is hard to get people to keep giving to a partnership once they are aware of the glitches—and there are always glitches! His advice was to build time limits into partnership—possibly three to five years, after which time there is a close examination of whether the partnership has been successful.

What Is True Collaboration?

Collaboration isn't just a distant conversation—two participants have to come pretty close to each other to form this type of relationship. In the very best collaborations, key staff members and volunteers form tight working relationships with each other, resulting in a synergy of purpose and a meshing together of gifts and abilities. In a true collaboration, the partners have to be transparent; hiding aspects of your organization or your work causes dysfunction. True collaboration is marked by sharing of resources, sharing of risk, and sharing of the glory of succeeding.

The following things can be said of a true collaboration:

- All partners express openly what it is they will gain from the collaboration. Everyone needs to gain something, or it isn't really collaboration. For example, partners might gain staff, access to a facility, or funds raised through jointly submitted grant proposals. I worked on one collaboration in which several start-up programs gained visibility and the goodwill of the community by partnering with a well-established and well-loved nonprofit in the community. The start-up groups stated openly at the beginning of the process that these were things they were hoping to gain.

- All partners contribute equally (as much as possible) to the collaboration. Everyone has to give something to make the collaboration work or there will be a sense of imbalance or unfairness in the collaboration from the start. Not every group has to give the same things to the partnership, but it should be clear that every group is giving something significant.

- It is clear who "owns" which aspects of the collaboration. This is where many collaborations fall apart. If your collaboration generates something—a curriculum or a program, for example, who owns what is generated? Talk about it at the outset, and include the ownership principles of the collaboration in the written agreement you put together.

- In a partnership involving a church congregation, there should be a sense of how the gifts within the body of Christ are being used and how the kingdom of God is being advanced through the collaboration. If you are working with a secular partner in your collaboration, you may have this conversation just among the people from your own congregation. As Christians, our motivations for collaborating need to extend beyond "what we can get" (money, fame, power) and focus instead on how well we serve and how the welfare of the community is advanced through the collaboration.

Kinds of Partners

Think creatively about the kinds of groups in your community that your church could partner with. Depending on how large your community is, there may be hundreds of possibilities! The kinds of partners you pursue will depend on the ministry dream of your congregation (see "Finding Your Congregation's Ministry Dream" in part 1) and your capacity as a congregation.

Possible partners might include the following:

- Public schools
- Youth mentoring program
- Nursing homes or assisted living facilities
- Nonprofits that construct affordable housing
- Local council of churches
- Environmental group working on sustainability issues
- Women's organizations
- Block club or neighborhood association
- Arts performance groups
- Veteran and military family support groups
- Local college or university

- Local youth development center
- Hospitals or clinics
- Community garden or local food co-op
- Preschool or early childhood center
- Animal shelter or animal welfare group
- Homeless shelter
- Food shelf or feeding program
- Athletic programs or recreation center
- Local business association
- Local senior center
- Workforce development center or job training program

Congregations that have been partnering with groups for years may have dozens of partners, but if your church is just starting to implement this model, choose just one or two partners to begin. This will give you a chance to try out what partnership is like for your church and develop an understanding of what your church brings to the table and where your gaps are.

Christ Presbyterian Church, a large congregation located in Edina, Minnesota, decided to streamline its partnership program after years of forming relationships with groups in the city. About ten years ago, CPC had nearly fifty partners, with partnership being defined mainly as the church providing financial support and limited volunteer participation. Mike Hotz, Associate Pastor of Urban/Local Engagement and Congregational Care at the church, described the transformation that the partnership program went through to achieve greater focus: "We took a hard look at our partnership program and decided that we were measuring success by the number of partners we had and the amount of money we gave away. We shifted to a focus on developing disciples instead, helping our church members engage Monday through Saturday in meaningful ways. We decided to set a high bar on the engagement of our volunteers—expecting them to be consistent and committed in their involvement. Ministry should not be part-time or episodic!"

Christ Presbyterian decided to focus on groups with the greatest involvement of CPC volunteers and to narrow its geographic focus to just a couple of areas of the city. They also began to do community collaborative-based partnerships, drawing together two or three of their partners into projects they could work on together. For example, an urban church partner lacked the resources to offer a large-scale youth program every week. Christ Presbyterian brought that church together with Young Life at a local park, where the three groups work together to serve a meal to a hundred community youth every week.

Choose Your Partners Wisely

One of the most critical steps to making this model a success is to choose your partner organizations wisely. Without the right partner, you could be sending your church members into a situation where they don't fit or could have a negative experience. In your search for a partner, you will want to find organizations that have the following characteristics:

They are ready to receive the number of volunteers your church can provide. Ask your potential partners how many volunteers they can reasonably handle, when they need them, and what they need them to do. You want to avoid a "size mismatch," for example, where you want to send fifty volunteers but the group can only handle ten. Make sure timing works as well. Daytime opportunities may not fit your congregation if your church members work 9:00 to 5:00 jobs.

They are working in an issue area that your church members are passionate about. If ideas for partnerships come only from church staff, it may be hard to get your church members excited about joining in. Find out what people in your congregation really care about and then look for partners that work in these issue areas. And you want to be sure that the kinds of skills your volunteers have are needed by the organization. For example, if you have a bunch of volunteers who like to swing a hammer, they may not be a good fit for a youth development organization that needs tutors to work one-on-one with kids. As described in Model 2, there is value in partnering with groups in which your church members are already involved—you'll have an inside contact who may help make conversations about partnership easier.

They are willing to create a positive experience for your volunteers. Find partners that are ready to create a gracious and positive environment for your volunteers. Look for a welcoming attitude on the part of people you meet with, as well as staff who have specific ideas about how they will use volunteers and support them. For example, the potential partner should have somebody who will communicate with your volunteers about scheduling issues, be available to answer their questions, and be on-site when they are there. There is nothing worse than volunteering and feeling like you have been set adrift, with no one around to talk to or get you what you need.

They are prepared to offer training or orientation for your volunteers. Volunteers need some type of training before jumping in with both feet. See Model 2: "Mobilize Volunteers" for more information on the kinds of training that might be beneficial for your volunteers to receive.

They are responsive to your need for communication. You want a partner who will communicate with you regularly, so you should look for groups that can follow through and respond to your emails and phone calls. You will get a sense of this as you begin to talk with a group about partnering. Does it take days and days to hear back from them, or are they pretty prompt in responding? Your expectations about communication could be something you discuss with a potential partner at the outset. If you decide to work with a very small nonprofit with limited staff, for example, asking them to give you a realistic estimate of how long it will take them to respond to phone messages and emails will help you keep your expectations in line with what is possible.

Ways to Partner

There are many ways to collaborate with another group—a few ideas are listed below. Many partnerships start in one or two areas and expand to include others.

Donate money or material goods. Many full-fledged partnerships start with donating money or goods to a partner. Strategies for donating are described in detail in Model 1.

Share space. You might consider sharing space with another organization if doing so would maximize your impact in the community. Some organizations like to set up an office or offer programming at a church building because churches are often easily accessible to people in the community. A partner could offer programming at your site or you could offer programs at theirs. Space sharing works best when you can develop a written agreement with your partner about who gets to use which space and when and who is responsible for cleaning and maintaining the space.

Mobilize volunteers. Sending volunteers to serve in a variety of capacities is a common aspect of partnership (described in detail in Model 2). Volunteers from your church could serve in front-line roles (ESL teachers, tutors, sports team coaches) or in more behind-the-scenes roles (office support, drivers, painters and fixers, etc.). Tightly partnered groups may send volunteers both ways—you help your partner out and they help you out. For example, your church may send volunteer mentors to serve at the local youth center, and perhaps youth and volunteers from the center come over to help out at the annual neighborhood festival sponsored by your church.

Refer program participants back and forth. Your collaboration could involve two or more organizations that provide complementary services to the community. No one organization in the collaboration provides everything that is needed, but when they put their services together, a continuum of services emerges that may help people get closer to achieving the goals they have set for themselves. For example, a program that places people in affordable housing needs to connect with other organizations that can provide food and clothing, job training, case management, and mental health services.

Plan programming together. Some collaborative partners sit at the table together regularly and dream about what is possible through the partnership and then make concrete plans together about how to do it. You might also get together to do activities to assess community issues and needs—walk the neighborhood or hear from a researcher from the university, for example, about a study of the community that has recently been completed.

Train together. Some partners attend staff development activities together. One of my current clients collaborates with the local neighborhood association, and the staff of both organizations recently participated in antiracism training together. With a larger group, it may be affordable for you to hire a trainer to develop customized training for you, or you might be able to get a group rate when attending a seminar or conference sponsored by someone else.

Share staff. Sharing staff is one of the more complex ways to partner, and you would need to work with your partner to clearly define the role of each shared staff person and who would be supervising that person while he or she is performing various duties. I have seen this work well for small churches that can't afford to hire a full-time youth minister but could share one with another congregation or nonprofit. In other instances, where space is also shared, two partners may share a staff person who has administrative or custodial duties for both organizations.

Fund-raise together. It may make sense to do some joint fundraising with your partner to secure resources for staff and program supplies and equipment. Many funders have a strong preference to fund collaborative efforts, with the idea that the end product is stronger when groups in a community work together. Here are a few rules of thumb to use when fund-raising together:

1. Clarify at the outset how much money each group will receive and what it is to be used for.
2. Clarify who is going to raise the money. Decide who will write the proposal; prepare the budgets and attachments; and something that groups often forget, write the reports at the end of the funding period.
3. Ensure that all partners sign off on the final version of the proposal before it is sent in to the funder.

Believers in Christ Church: Partnering with the Local Park

Believers in Christ Church, a congregation in North Minneapolis, developed the Eagles Wings Track Club in collaboration with Harrison Park, the public parks and recreation facility in the neighborhood near the church. Youth of all ages train at the park facilities and participate in a variety of track events, competing in eleven meets during the season (including regionals and nationals).

Eagles Wings was formed as the official track team for the park, and the team competes in meets through the Park Board circuit (and in the Junior Olympic circuit as well). The park provides training facilities and promotes the program through its communication channels. The church raises the funding for the program and operates it, including securing and supervising all of the coaches. The partnership provides the church with access to training facilities and a schedule of meets and also allows the park to offer a track program because of the people and funding provided by the church.

Believers in Christ first developed Eagles Wings because the pastor saw that some of the youth in the church's regular summer program "had a hard time sitting still!" "We wanted to serve as many youth as possible," said Pastor Joe Sutton, "and we saw that there were some who just needed to get out and move around a lot." The program has a strong family component—parents are encouraged to participate in warmups, attend meets, and even run in track events themselves at some of the meets.

Pastor Joe says one of the great benefits of the program is that it gets him out into the community in a role other than pastor. "Being out there running the program and coaching really gets me out of my 'pastoral bubble' and keeps me abreast of what is happening in the community."

"Hang Out and See What Happens": St. Michael's Lutheran Church Partners with the Local Townhome Complex

St. Michael's Lutheran Church in Bloomington, Minnesota, a first-ring suburb of the Twin Cities, partners with a local townhome complex to offer Kids Club in one of the townhome units on-site. The program serves a group of children and youth who have little to do after school, and many of them come from families living in poverty. The program operates out of one of the townhome units, providing after school programming one day a week to first through fifth graders living in the complex. Kids get homework help, participate in enrichment activities and games, and build a bond with volunteers from St. Michael's. In 2012 a middle school component was added to the program.

The idea for this community ministry came from Lori Wagner, a member of the church who lived in a townhome in the complex at the time. She noticed that there were "masses of kids" hanging around in the open spaces at the complex after school. Her study of cell groups and the changing demographics of the "mission field" in the Twin Cities helped give her a passion to create space in her life to pursue new ministry with her neighbors. She worked with

Sue Timmerman, the global missions coordinator at St. Michael's, to put together a Sunday school study about the potential for local ministry. Out of the class, a team of people stepped forward who were interested in building relationships at the townhomes to see what kind of ministry could arise.

The group started by just "hanging around" in Lori's backyard. "We told the people from our church just to sit and observe, and if you have the opportunity, interact with the neighbors. But our neighbors started interacting with us right away." The group decided to meet at Lori's place every other week during the summer and began offering simple activities for children—games of catch, face painting, craft projects, and puzzles. Some of the adults from St. Michael's began going door-to-door to talk to the neighbors, asking questions like "What do you like best about living here?" "What is a need you see in the area?" and "What can we pray for?" Sometimes the groups would only make it to six or seven units in an afternoon to talk to people, but they kept at it. The overwhelming response to the questions, according to Timmerman, was, "All these kids here have nothing focused for them to do."

After several months of programming, it became clear that running the program from Lori's home wasn't going to be sustainable. Then something wonderful happened—the manager of the property sent a letter to all residents asking whether there was anyone who could help with tutoring or provide other programming in the neighborhood. When the group from St. Michael's asked for a meeting with the property manager, they saw that a partnership was possible. "When we shared our dreams for the kids in our community, these were the same as her dreams for the kids," said Timmerman. "What we all wanted matched up and made the partnership possible." St. Michael's requested donated space from the property management company and was given space free of charge for the Kids Club program.

Consider this advice from St. Michael's on the partnership approach:

- Notice what is going on around you, build relationships, and start ministry based on that.
- Start something and see what happens!
- Start small and be sustainable and consistent.

- Communicate well from the beginning and show respect for each other.
- Be flexible. Your plan for the day may go out the window depending on who shows up for the program!

Communicate to the Congregation about the Partnership

Take every opportunity you can to communicate about your partnership to the congregation. Partnerships flourish because people enthusiastically support them. If only a few people in your congregation know (only the handful of volunteers who work on-site, for example), the partnership may flounder. This model will work best in your congregation if church staff are willing for the partnership to be highlighted through a variety of media.

Communication tools that you might use are outlined in Model 2 (see pages 63–64). When using the partnership model, you could add the following:

- Feature a link to your partner's website on your church's website.
- Invite your partner to make a presentation at regular church events, such as your annual dinner.
- Offer your partner a table at your church's ministry fair or missions fair if you have one.

Emphasize key messages about the partnership(s) when you communicate with your congregation, including information about the work of the partner organization, specifics about what the partnership involves (for example, sharing space or staff versus subsidizing expenses or recruiting volunteers), as well as educational information about the issue your partner works on. Here are some examples:

- Local hunger: statistics on how many families are "food insecure" and why.
- Sex trafficking: how youth and young adults get drawn into the sex trade and what is being done about it locally.
- Homelessness and affordable housing: how many people are homeless in your area and who they are, plus the kinds of aid that will really help them.

Most important, communicate with the congregation about opportunities for them to get involved. This can include regular volunteering, but also keep them informed about these things:

- How and what to donate
- Seasonal needs related to specific events
- How to help spread the word about the partnership with others in the church, community, and region

Keep Communicating and Assessing!

Once you have formed a collaboration, the work (and the fun) have just begun. Set regular times for key staff and volunteers to get together and have honest conversations about how things are going. Evaluate your progress against the outcomes you set at the beginning of the process. Is the collaboration resulting in something significant for the community?—that is the key question. But also take time to talk about the "nuts and bolts" of how the collaboration works. Are services being delivered well? Are volunteers being placed? Are administrative details being taken care of (paperwork, etc.)? Is communication between the partners strong? These are the kinds of questions that will help you to strengthen your partnership over time and increase its impact in the community.

What You'll Need

- An awareness of what kind of partner you are looking for
- One or more partner organizations seeking a good match with your church
- People in the church who will advocate for the partnership
- Identified ways to connect with your partner(s)
- Written agreements, even if they are simple ones, spelling out the elements of the partnership
- Tools to communicate about the partnership to the congregation and the willingness to use some of the communication space at the church to highlight the partnership

MODEL 4

Advocate around Public Policy*

WHAT IT IS: *Your congregation advocates for (or against) public policies that affect a community or people you care about. Your work could focus at the federal, state, or local level, or all three, depending on which issues you choose. This work is frequently done in partnership with nonprofit organizations that provide education and training to congregations on how to influence the public policy process and that also provide opportunities to take action.*

Let Justice Roll Down

This is what the LORD Almighty said: "Administer true justice; show mercy and compassion to one another." —ZECHARIAH 7:9, NIV

To truly follow God means that we can never escape the idea of justice. It was one of God's main admonitions to the children of Israel—to be just in dealing with everyone, especially widows and orphans. Practicing justice is described throughout Scripture as one mark of being a true follower of God.

---

*My thanks to Alison Killeen, statewide organizer for the Joint Religious Legislative Coalition, for her advice in writing this chapter.

And it is not just temporary or surface justice that God is interested in—this is long-standing, deep, and structural justice that sets wrongs right and frees the disenfranchised from the systems that enslave them. We can see this in the idea of the year of Jubilee that God commanded the nation of Israel to practice every forty-nine years.

In that year, property returned to its original owners, and God made a point of saying that the Israelites shouldn't cheat each other. How the land was to be priced was spelled out in detail, the idea being that any small injustices that people had done to each other over the years would now be righted. It was change at the very root of the system, not just a rearranging of the pieces on the same game board. It was an all new game board!

Getting at the root of the matter is one hallmark of public policy advocacy. People of faith come together to ask the question "What is causing this injustice, and how can we work to change it at the structural level?" Working for this deep change is working for something that is close to God's heart.

The Value of Public Policy Advocacy

One of the primary benefits of this advocating for public policy model is that it helps draw your church into changing the system, not just responding to the results of that system. Churches who use this model say they like working on the root causes, because doing so has the potential to bring about more permanent change in society and in people's lives. Sometimes congregations turn here when they become frustrated after years of doing front-line work and seeing the effects of a broken system on children and families. For example, if your church partners with a homeless shelter and you find that many of the homeless are people with mental health issues who can't receive insurance coverage for their medications, you might investigate how those insurance programs are structured and find a way to advocate for change.

High crime and substandard housing in your community might lead you to look at housing laws and advocate for change on how absentee landlords run their properties. Your experiences with children who can't read might lead you to look more closely at the public schools. As a result, church members might decide to advocate for the upcoming property tax levy that will benefit the schools.

Another advantage here is that the advocacy process typically involves extensive education on the issue you choose. Particularly if you partner with an advocacy-focused nonprofit, your church members can be educated by experts on a variety of issues. As a church, you could learn all about health care at public hospitals, laws governing the sale of handguns, access to preschool education, and public funding for the arts—just to name a few topics. You could become "experts" on an issue you care about and use that expertise in years to come in your community ministry efforts. But note that while education can be a wonderful benefit to this model, it can be challenging as well. Gathering facts and information about some public policy issues can be difficult. And depending on the level of interest in your congregation, it could be challenging to get church members to attend educational sessions.

Being engaged in this model may also lead church members to become more engaged in the political process over the long term, even after your work as a church on a particular legislative issue is done. Understanding how the political process actually works can be very empowering to people, and seeing how their efforts influenced change can inspire further action.

Another real advantage of this approach is that public policy efforts often draw people of different faiths, denominations, and ethnic groups together. Many advocacy networks (described later in this chapter) are interfaith, bringing Christians, Muslims, Jews, and people of other religions together to work on an issue. Even networks that include just Christians may involve people from mainline, evangelical, African American, immigrant, and independent churches, as well as many others.

In a diverse network like this, you are learning about much more than just the issue at hand—you are learning about another culture, another faith, another way of life. People I interviewed for this book described how much joy it brings Christian participants in the process when they meet someone of like mind on an issue who just happens to be Jewish, for example. Your church members may come away from this process with a much deeper understanding of and appreciation for the different types of people who live in your community.

Challenges of the Advocacy Model

This community ministry model may be too "political" for some. Depending on your denominational background or religious tradition, church members may see politics as something that is (and needs to be) completely separate from the church. Even if you choose issues that are not politically charged or controversial, church members may have a hard time embracing this model if they are used to thinking of church as being "over here" and political activity as something far removed from faith life—something that is "over there." If you like a challenge and think you can convince church members eventually, you might start this process by developing a theology of public engagement, with some teaching and preaching on how Christians can and should engage with the broader society.

Politically divided congregations may also have difficulty implementing this model. If you think about the political affiliations of your church members and you are hard-pressed to come up with one direction they "lean," it may be hard to land on one side of an issue together. The model may also be difficult for you to implement if there is a great deal of "antigovernment" sentiment within your congregation. Some Americans hold the view (and right now it seems to be a popular one) that any form of government program, expenditure, or intervention is bad. If you have a number of people like this in your church, it may be difficult to convince them that spending time and energy learning how to make government act justly is a worthwhile endeavor.

Another challenge is that you won't always win. Several church leaders told me about the roller-coaster feeling experienced with this model. Your congregation will feel exhilarated when your efforts produce real change but will probably be discouraged when legislative issues they worked so hard on don't come through. These inevitable ups and downs in the process can make it hard to sustain interest and momentum in your advocacy efforts. One way to address the roller coaster is to build advocacy into your church culture (see the following) so that it becomes a matter of course in church life.

St. Mark's Sioux Falls: A Focus on Alleviating Hunger

St. Mark's Lutheran Church in Sioux Falls, South Dakota, has had a longtime focus on helping to alleviate hunger in the community. The church uses a hybrid model (see "Choosing a Model for Ministry," pages 143–158) that involves raising funds for the Evangelical Lutheran Church in America's hunger appeal and collecting food for the local food shelf (Model 1) and participating in public policy advocacy activities (Model 4), mainly through involvement with Bread for the World. According to Cathy Brechtelsbauer, chair of the mission committee at the church and the Bread for the World coordinator for South Dakota, using several approaches is important because "our local food shelf could never handle the need if the federal food programs were reduced or eliminated. We need all of these resources for hungry people."

The church has Bread for the World–themed Sundays twice a year, with hunger highlighted in worship in some way. One year the pastor taught the Gospel lesson on the parable of the woman who mixed yeast into a large quantity of flour to make bread (Matthew 13:33; Luke 13:20-21), and during the sermon, one of the teens from the church dragged a fifty-pound bag of flour up onto the stage (slightly less than the amount of flour the woman in the story was working with). Another year, bread-making machines were set up in the back of the church, and the smell of baking bread wafted through the sanctuary during the service, drawing attention to hunger.

Once a year, the worship service includes an "Offering of Letters." In 2012 a skit during the service used twenty grocery bags to represent all the food assistance in the United States. Nineteen of them represented public programs! Four speakers from the congregation used the skit to explain the importance of the "Circle of Protection," the focus of Bread for the World's Offering of Letters in 2012:

- Poverty-focused development assistance focused on poor countries around the world
- International food aid
- Tax credits for low-income families in the United States
- Nutrition programs here in the United States

On this letter-writing Sunday, church members are provided with written materials on how to write a letter to their public officials. Letter-writing tips are provided as well as a sample letter for reference. Letter writers are encouraged to ask for specific action and to give a reason or two for why they are writing.

A key to the success of St. Mark's advocacy efforts has been to highlight stories of the concrete impact that is being made as a result of the work. Bread for the World often has international advocacy goals, and one year a goal was debt relief for third world countries. The World Bank and IMF were asked to forgive the debts of extremely poor nations, thus freeing up resources within each nation for education, housing, and other resources to address poverty. Because of debt relief, many countries were able to drop school fees, making it possible for millions more children to attend school. In one village in Cameroon, an extension was built on the school to house the growing group of students. When church members from St. Mark's visited the village on a mission trip, they saw the expanded school and heard stories from villagers about the larger group of students and then carried those stories back to St. Mark's to share with the congregation. Brechtelsbauer said she uses a photo of the expanded school to remind church members about the impact their letters made.

Types of Activities

Churches engage in public policy advocacy through a variety of activities. Some congregations choose one or two activities; others participate in an entire continuum of advocacy that runs from simple activities to more complex and time-consuming ones. Churches often start with those that require less time or engagement—such as attending an educational session or writing a letter—and then ramp up to include things like attending meetings with a number of public officials.

Here is an overview of the kinds of activities that your church could engage in if you are interested in public policy advocacy:

Educational sessions for your congregation. Many churches start here, with educational forums (often on a Sunday morning) about the advocacy process or the issues the congregation would like to address. Education can help church members change their minds (or become passionate about) the church's role in challenging systems and people in power. Education can also help members catch the vision for the difference they could make on a particular issue. Through a forum, they might learn about the realities facing disenfranchised people in your community—the homeless, veterans, returning citizens, or youth who have been trafficked, for example.

Alison Killeen of the Joint Religious Legislative Coalition said that staff members from her group frequently present at "adult forums" at churches: "We usually begin with the larger view—'How does my faith relate to public life? What can I do to help change the structures that cause injustice?' And then we talk about one or more specific issues where they could take action. For example, with child poverty, we will discuss the research that shows how lack of income affects child brain development, then highlight policies that could affect children's well-being—funding for child care, for example, and school lunches."

An offering of letters. This is one of the more popular ways that churches engage in advocacy, and many congregations around the country include this as a regular part of worship or other church events. Church members are asked to write letters to public officials on a particular topic or piece of legislation. You can provide sample letters to your members that they can use as a template, or you might simply provide them with some key information and ask them to write their own letters.

People I interviewed for this book said that where the letter-writing table is placed and when and where letter writing is encouraged has a significant impact on the level of participation. If you highlight letter writing as part of a worship service, you will have higher participation. If you place the letter-writing table in a prominent position as people enter or leave the sanctuary, you will have higher participation. One church I interviewed said they moved the Sunday morning donuts to the letter table and had higher participation then ever! Another church said they placed the table literally in front of the exit to the sanctuary—you had to go around the table to get out of the church! Many more people stopped to write a letter when the table was in such a prominent position.

Church members have also said that letter writing can be a great way for children and teens to get engaged in the advocacy process. One church enticed children with brownies. The kids asked, "If we write a letter, may we have a brownie?" But then they spent so much time writing letters, they didn't have time to eat the brownies! Another church sponsored a pizza party for teens. Each of the girls who attended had researched the public policy topics carefully. They shared information and ideas with each other then wrote twelve letters each!

Meet with your public officials. Meeting face-to-face with public officials to talk to them about an issue is another popular advocacy strategy. This could be part of a Day on the Hill or on your own. Your advocacy partner organization (see "Seek a Partner to Help You Build Your Program" at right) might arrange an annual Day on the Hill in your community, providing an opportunity for church members to meet with their own state legislator to discuss an issue. Training is often provided in advance so participants know how to have the conversation. Or you might decide to arrange these meetings on your own. Prayer is often a key aspect of preparing for these meetings. Identifying and learning about the public officials involved can help you know how to pray for them and their involvement in the issue you have chosen.

It is important to focus on officials from the district where your church is located or from the districts where church members live. In the office of a public official, constituents rule! But people from outside the district usually get little attention.

Results can be significant. There are many stories of officials who changed their minds on key legislation because clergy or church leaders came to see them. Also important for your church members, being a part of a Day on the Hill experience can help them more fully understand the political process and be less intimidated about approaching public officials in the future.

Sign petitions. Some churches participate in petition drives, working toward getting hundreds or even thousands of signatures on a petition, which is then presented to one or more public officials to show strong public support for or opposition to proposed legislation.

Hold special events. Special events that highlight your issue might also be a part of your advocacy effort. Interfaith Power and Light, a national campaign of the Regeneration Project, engages congregations and faith leaders in public policy issues related to global warming. IPL organizes a preach-in every year held on the weekend closest to Valentine's Day. The theme is "Love Creation and Love Your Neighbor." Interfaith Power and Light provides sample sermons for preachers who want them and provides postcards for congregants to send to their public officials on a key legislative issue advocating for clean air or tighter regulation on greenhouse gases (see full description of IPL's work below). In partnership with 350.org, IPL encouraged their member congregations to ring their bells 350 times in a row, to remind people of the parts per million of carbon dioxide that is the recommended maximum level. Rev. Sally Bingham, the founder of Interfaith Power and Light, described the motivation behind these special events and other IPL activities: "People of faith have a moral responsibility to protect creation. If we don't, how can we ask others to do it?"

Use the media to advocate for an issue. Members of your congregation might choose to highlight your issue in the media by writing letters to the editor, submitting op-eds, or participating in radio interviews or holding press conferences. If you partner with an advocacy group, they may provide you with sample op-eds or letters, or a list of facts that would be good to include in your letter to the editor.

Seek a Partner to Help You Build Your Program

Rather than trying to launch a "do-it-yourself" advocacy effort in your church, you could look for a national or local advocacy organization that can provide resources for your congregation as you plan and move ahead. Some advocacy organizations are organized around a single hot-button issue, such as abortion, immigration, or the death penalty. Others focus on a constellation of related issues, such as poverty, unemployment, the environment, or rights for a particular group of people.

Organizations such as Bread for the World and Interfaith Power and Light are national organizations that focus, respectively, on reducing hunger and poverty and protecting the environment. Both groups provide tools and templates that can help your congregation engage in the public policy process. As I said above, Interfaith Power and Light engages congregations and faith leaders in public policy issues related to global warming. They also provide tools and resources to help congregations become "greener" by using renewable energy, increasing energy efficiency, and creating more climate-friendly grounds. As described in the ministry profile of St.

Mark's Church on page 85, Bread for the World chooses a legislative theme each year related to reducing hunger and poverty in the United States and around the world.

Many local communities also have advocacy networks that could be a real help to you. Minnesota's Joint Religious Legislative Coalition is an example of a group like this. It is an interfaith, statewide advocacy coalition that lobbies at the Minnesota state legislature and organizes around issues of social justice. The four sponsors of the coalition are Minnesota Council of Churches, the Islamic Center, the Jewish Community Relations Council, and the Minnesota Catholic Conference. In 2013, JRLC pushed for the Family Economic Security Act, a bill that would raise the minimum wage, expand the child care assistance program, and expand tax credits.

The value of seeking a partner is that you don't have to do all of the public policy research from scratch, decipher the legislative process, create the tools (like letters), arrange and schedule events, or manage a host of other small details—your partner can probably do that for you. You just need to get your church members engaged. A partner advocacy organization might provide the following helps for you:

- Detailed written information on legislation or the political process that you can share with your congregation
- Speakers for an educational session for your congregation or curriculum that you can use to teach it yourself. Some groups even have outlines or curriculum for Bible studies or sermons
- Arrange a Day on the Hill (either in your community or in Washington, DC) that your church members can attend and provide training beforehand
- Arrange other types of events
- Sample letters for a letter-writing campaign, sample op-eds and letters to the editor, postcards, petitions
- Periodic legislative updates: meetings, webinars, conference calls or emails with progress updates on the legislative issue you are working on
- Connections with other congregations that are doing advocacy work and working on the same issues

Getting Started

Form a small group of people who are passionate about advocacy work. Advocacy work often starts with just a small group of people in a congregation (even two or three in some cases) and is often sustained by the passion of those few people. Unlike planning groups you might utilize to get other models going, this group will be critical to not just launching your public policy effort but sustaining it too. They will likely be the people to arrange educational sessions for the congregation, work with your advocacy partner, coordinate advocacy activities, and communicate about the work.

Establish strong theological underpinnings for engaging in public policy work. The strongest advocacy work in churches is grounded in Scripture. The work we do as people of faith is different from the work of secular advocacy groups. We are motivated by God's call to address injustice at the structural level, as demonstrated in Scripture passages like Isaiah 58:6-7: "Is this not the fast that I choose: to loose the bonds of injustice, to undo the thongs of the yoke, to let the oppressed go free, and to break every yoke? Is it not to share your bread with the hungry, and bring the homeless poor into your house. . . ?"

Deuteronomy 10:17-19 is another strong text on justice for the orphan, widow, and stranger: "For the LORD your God is God of gods and Lord of lords, the great God, mighty and awesome, who is not partial and takes no bribe, who executes justice for the orphan and the widow, and who loves the strangers, providing them food and clothing. You shall also love the stranger, for you were strangers in the land of Egypt." Other compelling Scriptures include Amos 5:18-24 (especially verse 24) and Matthew 25:31-46.

It is important for church members to see advocacy as a spiritual act that is connected to their faith, not just secular involvement in politics, like volunteering for a political campaign. That way, when you encounter opposition or bumps in the road, the congregation's commitment to the work runs deep.

Choose an issue or a set of issues. Some congregations start the entire advocacy process with an issue that at least a few people in your church are passionate about and one that draws others forward into advocacy (funding for local public schools, for example, or the voter ID amendment on your state ballot). In contrast, some churches don't choose an issue until they are quite a ways down the advocacy road (later in the process). Church members have a passion for getting at the root of injustice but don't have particular issues in mind until more members from the congregation get engaged in the discussion.

If this is your first time participating in advocacy, steer clear of controversial issues—focus on ones that most people in your congregation could support. Many congregations focus on hunger or some other human need the first time out. This will help you build support for the idea of advocacy over the long term as people learn the advocacy ropes.

Building Momentum

Gain broader support. Your efforts will be most successful if your senior pastor supports what you are doing and can advocate publicly, including from the pulpit, for the issues and the theological significance of the work you are doing. You will also need to decide early on whether to seek the support of the entire congregation (perhaps through a congregational resolution) before proceeding with public policy advocacy. This kind of consensus often provides the momentum that a new advocacy effort needs to really take off at the start and to keep going over time if your efforts don't result in the change you had hoped for.

Build relationships within the congregation. Building relationships and spending time talking are important practices in building an advocacy program and sustaining it. Once a core group of people has formed, many congregations launch an intentional campaign to have one-on-one conversations with one another. (This is a core aspect of community organizing as well—see Model 5). Questions to ask one another might include: "What do you believe Jesus calls us to do in the world?" "What are some of your favorite passages in the Bible about justice and mercy?" "Where have you seen instances that you wanted to change the root causes or structures in order to bring about greater justice in the world?" "Have you wondered what a further step would be?"

One staff member of an advocacy nonprofit said, "The conversations help connect people to the root of the problem. They can be motivational and almost intimate—really helping people get to know each other. Talking like this helps us get at the root of what we hold dear—what we are called to do."

Finally, the conversations need to have a distinct "ask"—inviting people to participate, asking them how they (specifically) would like to help out.

Train and equip the congregation. Creative opportunities for church members to learn about issues and advocacy will help your advocacy campaign succeed. See "Educational sessions for your congregation" (pages 86–87) for specific ideas.

Sustaining Involvement

Make advocacy part of your church culture. If your church is interested in sticking with advocacy over the long term (rather than just gearing up for a single initiative), find ways to incorporate advocacy into the culture of your congregation. Rather than being a huge, occasional project that happens just once or twice a year, advocacy may become habitual for your congregation. Education efforts are ongoing, advocacy is highlighted from the pulpit and through other communication means on a regular basis, and church members are called to action on a regular basis.

Communicate with your congregation year-round. This will keep your issues and the idea of advocacy in front of them. Use multiple communication tools to reach the most people. Blurbs in the bulletin and articles in the church newsletter can work well. You may also want to use an "action table" put in a prominent place that everyone needs to walk by. Some churches have Advocacy Sunday once a month or quarter—a chance to share information about the issue, what has changed, and opportunities to engage. Regular Facebook updates and a Twitter feed can help keep people updated as well. If you win on your issue, make sure to celebrate and communicate that in multiple ways to the congregation. Victories can help ensure that more people will want to get involved next time.

Advocacy Works in a Wide Range of Churches

Public policy advocacy isn't just for highly educated, politically literate congregations or for churches that have a history with this model. In my research, I encountered a number of congregations that were trying advocacy for the first time quite successfully. And a real diversity of churches pursue this model. Congregations from a range of denominations are involved, as well as a diversity of churches when it comes to ethnicity, income level, and education level. So don't assume this model isn't for you if your congregation has never tried it or because your church members are political neophytes. If your congregation is passionate about changing the causes of injustice, this may be the model for you.

What You'll Need

- A small group of members who are passionate about your church being engaged in advocacy
- An issue or set of issues that your church can get behind
- A partner organization that can provide tools such as education materials, speakers, and training
- A willingness on the part of leaders to set aside time and space in worship services and at other times when the congregation gathers to talk about advocacy and the issues you have chosen

MODEL 5

Engage in Community Organizing*

WHAT IT IS: *Building relationships with people in your church and in your community so that you can take collective action on an issue of injustice. While this model has themes and tactics in common with Models 3 and 4, community organizing is unique in that it typically involves empowerment of the people most affected by the issues being addressed—they are an important part of the coalitions that are formed. Also, actions in community organizing aren't limited to the public policy arena—a broader range of actions are used, including rallies, use of the media, and more confrontational tactics such as protests and boycotts. Another important distinction is that organizing efforts focus on building coalitions that will act together over the long term rather than just focusing on a single issue or action and then disbanding.*

All Together Now

The book of Nehemiah is an endless source of inspiration to me. Nehemiah was called by God to return a great distance to the spiritual home of his people to repair the broken-down walls of the city.

---

*My thanks to Matt McDermott, lead organizer, Congregations Organized for a New Connecticut (CONECT), for his advice in writing this chapter.

He examined the situation carefully then called all of the people to work: "Then I said to them, 'You see the trouble we are in, how Jerusalem lies in ruins with its gates burned. Come, let us rebuild the wall of Jerusalem, so that we no longer suffer disgrace'" (2:17).

In his call to the people, Nehemiah was calling all of the people. Nehemiah 3 provides a detailed description of who was there to do the work: nobles, priests, artisans, gatekeepers, public officials, and temple servants. And it is important to note that while the rebuilders included people from far away, many were those who lived adjacent to the part of the wall they were repairing. So the people living in the broken-down situation—who had seen, heard, and experienced it all—were instrumental in repairing it. This great diversity of people makes me think of the diverse coalitions that gather in community organizing. Organizing typically includes in the coalition the people who are most affected by the injustice. They are trained as leaders and empowered to work toward change just like the people who come from "outside" the situation. What better way to live out our faith than to call all of the people to the work, just as Nehemiah did.

Advantages of Community Organizing

Like advocating for public policy, this model tends to focus on root causes, pushing for bigger change that gets at the policies, practices, and ways of doing business that cause injustices. One organizer said that organizing allows congregations to "operate on a bigger stage to act on and learn from. They are acting together with other congregations, power figures, and public officials to bring about change."

One of the hallmarks of community organizing is building relationships, both within the congregation and with people outside of it. While relationship building is a part of many of the models in this book, what makes it different in community organizing is that it is an intentional and formal part of the process. The focus is on building relationships to form coalitions around issues.

As a part of your community organizing effort, training may be provided on the art of the one-on-one conversation—sitting down with another person to talk about what is important to you, what you are passionate about, and what you see as key community issues. One organizer told me, "People may have been in the same church for fifty years, but this is the first time they sit down together to have a meaningful conversation. These kinds of conversations don't happen during coffee hour or in committee work; you need to create a space for them to happen."

Conversations may take just fifteen minutes and are designed to get people talking about themselves. The two people involved in the "one-on-ones" will be given a preset list of questions, designed to get people talking about what is important to them, what motivates them, and the assets they possess. Here are some sample questions from churches I interviewed:

- What brings you the most joy in your work?
- What kind of impact do you want to have?
- What is the biggest challenge you have faced in your life? And how does it still affect you?
- What accomplishments or project are you proudest of?
- What did you learn (especially about yourself) in the conversational process?

Your organizing work may also include one-on-one conversations with people in your community. You might decide to ask these same questions of residents, business owners, staff at the local public school or park, nonprofit leaders, city officials, youth, parents, seniors, and _____ (you fill in the blank). One organizer told me that in his work with immigrant communities, it wasn't possible to walk right up to people and start asking them questions about their concerns. Instead, his group helped form soccer teams, getting to know both youth and their parents during practices and games. Trust was built, and parents spoke more freely once they had gotten to know the people with the organizing group. This group has also used community gardens in a similar way. The organizer said, "It is easier to talk when you are sharing vegetables over your back fence!"

Community organizing also encourages extensive research into issues, with the idea that before you are able to take effective action; you need to know the issue inside and out. Before Holy Trinity Lutheran Church developed a strategy for taking on the payday loan establishments in their neighborhood (see "Choosing a Model for Ministry," pages 147–149), several members read every book and article on the issue they could get their hands on. An attorney with expertise in predatory lending provided a great deal of information as well. The church is also working to collect stories from people in the neighborhood about their use of these businesses. Church members are attempting to talk with people as they enter or exit one of the establishments, distributing a brochure that asks community residents if they would be willing to drop by or call the church to share about their experience. In the process, a number of people in the church have become much more well-informed about what is happening in their community.

Another benefit of participating in community organizing is that leaders are developed—participants learn how to strategize, plan, lead meetings, talk about issues, and conduct research. A number of the church leaders I spoke with described how developing new leaders through organizing efforts helped their church in many other ways as well. People in the church who had been more in the background were now equipped as leaders and had the confidence and skills to take charge of a church committee or ministry task force or serve on the church board.

Another benefit to this model: collective community organizing efforts are often cross-denominational and interfaith, meaning that people in your congregation will have the chance to get to know people who believe differently than they do. People I interviewed for this chapter emphasized the first-time opportunities that many church members had to talk to someone of another faith and build a relationship.

Challenges of Community Organizing

Similar to the challenges of advocating for public policy, one downside of community organizing is that change can be slow, and this may be frustrating to congregation members who are impatient to see (almost) immediate results to their hard work. If you have lofty goals (that is not unusual in an organizing effort) and are working for change in very large institutions (also not unusual), you might find that you are chipping away at your agenda for a long period of time, encountering both successes and setbacks. Help your congregation orient their expectations properly (communicate often that this is a long haul), and be sure to celebrate small successes along the way.

Community organizing can also be incredibly time-consuming. Because organizing is often done in a large group of people with a number of institutions involved, the group needs to be trained, make decisions together about what to focus on, organize relationship-building efforts and events (like rallies or meetings with legislators), and keep all of that going over a long period of time. One pastor told me that he spends three or four days a month or more on community organizing efforts and that he has to have many conversations in order to get even a few people in the church involved.

As with public policy advocacy, this model may be difficult to implement for congregations with many members who feel the church has no place in public life—believing Christians should not be engaged in taking on people and institutions with power. That said, moving forward on this model can also be an opportunity to teach about the biblical roots of engaging with power and political systems. A pastor who leads community organizing efforts in the Bronx, New York, says, "On nearly every page and in every chapter of the Bible, there is political engagement: the prophet speaking to the king and religious and military leaders; Israel resisting being taken over by another political power; Daniel saying to the king, 'I won't eat from your table.' All of these things that we are dealing with in our context are there in Scripture." If you think community organizing is the right model for your congregation despite some opposition like this, you could initiate a fruitful conversation on the Christian's role in public life.

Community organizing may also be considered a higher risk model than some of the others because some of the confrontational tactics that can be part of an organizing effort may bring greater (negative) public visibility to your church. Even if most of your church members agree with the idea of taking on the powers that be, some of the more confrontational tactics used in community organizing may be hard for some church members to get behind. Be sure to understand what types of action your congregation would be most likely to want to participate in before you sign everyone up for protests, picketing, or civil disobedience that may result in folks getting arrested!

If you choose a community organizing partner that will provide training and coordinate action, be sure you understand whether they will be using confrontational tactics. There are many styles and tactics in community organizing. I interviewed people who used a quiet, behind-the-scenes approach—networking, building relationships, meeting with officials, and applying more "quiet" pressure to effect change. I also talked with groups that were apt to chain themselves to corporate headquarters and shout down officials at large public meetings. Early in the process, be sure to inform yourself about the tactics used by a potential partner and understand how your church members would want to participate.

Another potential challenge is that community organizing coalitions typically require their member organizations to pay dues. The amount varies depending on the group and on the size of your congregation (dues are usually based in part on the number of church members), but the amount is usually more than nominal. One organizing group I talked to had fees that ranged from $500 (smallest church) to $12,000 (largest church). So if money is very tight or it is difficult to get anything new into the church budget, this may not be the model for you.

What Kind of Change Are We Organizing For?

Unlike public policy advocacy, in which the change being pushed for is legislative and focused on what government can do, the change pushed for in community organizing efforts can focus on much more than public policy. Groups that are working together in community organizing might pull together to try to accomplish the following goals.

Change in How Businesses and Corporations Operate

Your community organizing efforts may be focused on getting businesses or corporations in your community to change their practices. For example, some community organizing groups fight against "redlining" by banks—the practice of excluding certain institutions and people from receiving bank financing because of who they are and where they live. Redlining can severely limit growth in a community. Lack of access to cash prevents people from buying or improving homes in the community; businesses can't get financing to expand or make improvements, and nonprofits might not be able to get loans to purchase or build buildings.

Change in How Government Institutions Operate

Community organizing might include a legislative focus (similar to the public policy model), working with local, state, or federal legislative bodies to pass or repeal laws or to change regulations. This could include your city or town council, county board, state legislature, or congressional representatives. Your focus could also be on the executive or judicial branches of government. In cities with a strong mayoral system, the focus would be less on the city council and much more on the mayor's decisions. City or state departments might also be a focus. Examples could include your state's Veteran Affairs Department (in how they administrate benefits for vets), your city's Housing and Economic Development Department (more equity in how funding for new housing projects is dispersed), or the U.S. Department of Agriculture (preventing cuts in food programs for the poor).

Change in How Other Institutions Operate

Other major institutions in a community, such as a hospital or school, may also be the focus of community organizing efforts. A number of communities around the United States have organized to push change in the "charity care" policies of local hospitals— people being denied care because of their perceived inability to pay. Organizing efforts focused on school districts might push for special services for a certain population of students or improved schools in one part of the district.

Establishing New Programs or Organizations to Respond to Community Need

Sometimes community organizing efforts identify a gap that is not being met by others and perhaps can't be for a variety of reasons. The identification of this gap might lead groups to develop their own programs or organizations in response. For example, if you are working to change how banks interact with their community, your church might decide to pull together with other congregations or groups to open your own credit union to better provide lower-cost financing and bank services for residents. Affiliates of a national community organizing group started Nehemiah Homes—new community development corporations in Baltimore and New York City that build affordable single-family homes and townhomes.

Lake County United: Organizing Congregations to Effect Real Change

Lake County United is an affiliate of the Industrial Areas Foundation working in Lake County, Illinois. Comprised of member faith communities and nonprofits, the organization brings its members together to work for "a just society through active citizenship." A wide range of congregations participate, including those from Episcopal, Catholic, Presbyterian, Lutheran, Methodist, Unitarian, Jewish, Muslim, and evangelical traditions as well as nonprofit organizations.

When Lake County United first began the listening and relationship-building process in Waukegan, Illinois, staff members were convinced that the main issue would be immigration since there had been a major demographic shift with many Latino immigrants moving into the community in recent years. Staff were surprised when concerns about the public education system made the top of the list. Many families came to the United States to see their children advance and were frustrated by the significant high school dropout rate among Latino students and their low ACT scores. Some students were going on to community college, needing to take a full year of remedial classes before they could begin their course of study.

Working with their member institutions and other residents, Lake County United devised a plan to start a college-prep charter high school that would better meet the needs of students who were struggling in the district's public schools. More than nine hundred residents turned out for a "public action" to unveil the proposal for the new school and to ask questions of school board members. However, the school district lined up as "utterly opposed," according to Matt McDermott, former lead organizer for Lake County

United. "When the school board voted down our charter school proposal, we had to ask ourselves, 'What could we do without the permission of the school board?'"

Then the group from Lake County United came up with the idea of starting its own college readiness program—Waukegan to College. The program was initially operated by Lake County United but has now been spun off into its own nonprofit organization. The students who participate in the program come from ten member institutions of Lake County United in Waukegan, mostly member congregations. The program includes one-on-one tutoring, individual family counseling, an academic coach for each student, and advocacy within the school system, to make sure students are enrolled in challenging courses that fit their abilities. Volunteers from other Lake County United member institutions are serving as tutors and mentors in the program. Through Waukegan to College, parents are learning how to help their children succeed in high school and navigate the college application process. Students are receiving the support they need to prepare for their college careers.

General Elements of Community Organizing

There are many styles and types of community organizing, but all of the approaches have the following elements in common.

Inclusive of Many Different People and Institutions

In particular, community organizing includes those impacted by injustice. As noted in the opening pages of this chapter, this element is a unique aspect of organizing that sets it apart from the other community ministry models in this book. In organizing there is an intentional effort to empower the people most affected by the injustice to have a loud and strong voice in the process.

For example, in community organizing efforts, standing alongside clergy, nonprofit and neighborhood leaders, union activists, and concerned citizens might be the actual victims of bank redlining, people personally denied service by the local hospital, laborers directly affected by budget cuts, and those who have themselves been treated unjustly by the courts. One organizer told me that including youth and parents in their work to get the school district to enhance services for non-English-speaking students made district officials more accountable. The presence of students and parents made it more difficult for officials to dismiss the initiative with "Students don't want to learn" or "Parents don't care."

Focus on Relationships and Research

Before settling on an issue or specific action strategies, a significant amount of time is spent building relationships—both inside the congregation and with people in the broader community. This strategy is described in detail earlier in the chapter, but in a real sense, this relationship building also reflects the model's focus on research.

Community organizing efforts usually include a focus on in-depth research, gathering as much information as possible about the issue at hand. Research helps make the case for or against your issue as you are meeting with and writing to people in power, and it may bring to light facts that were previously unknown to decision makers. One organizer suggested starting the research process by asking, "What questions do we need to get answered to know this issue inside and out?" Details on how you might conduct research are described earlier in this chapter.

Leadership Development

Organizing efforts focus on the development of grassroots leaders, many of whom are "nonexperts." Matt McDermott of Congregations Organized for a New Connecticut said, "These are not lawyers or doctors; they are average citizens who become versed on public life, developing themselves and their own skills and power to be able to shape their own lives, their own congregation, and their own community." Grassroots leaders will learn about building relationships, running meetings (keep them focused on action, not just making reports), implementing small group techniques, and using strategies for getting things done and getting them done in a timely fashion, among many other skills. These are techniques and tools that can transfer into running the church council or a church committee and any number of other leadership roles in the church and community.

Focus on Key Issues

Organizing involves targeting one or more key issues for action, the more specific the better. Some organizing coalitions focus more on the big picture, taking a symbolic stance on an issue ("Everyone should have access to health care"), but groups that have achieved the greatest number of "wins" have typically broken bigger issues down into smaller pieces, so that coalition members were advocating for specific legislation or other action (for example, allowing children to remain on their parents' health insurance until age twenty-six).

One organizer said that in an organizing effort focused on cleaning up problem rental properties in one neighborhood, "instead of saying to the city council, 'Clean up all these houses now!' we decided to focus on thirty properties." He said that city officials were more responsive to this focused approach. Each block club in the neighborhood was asked to identify one property on their block that needed attention. The result of the effort was that twenty-three problem properties in the neighborhood were cleaned up.

Understanding Who Has the Power

In organizing, an effort must be made to understand how things really get done—who is the real decision maker or influencer in a situation? In many institutions there is a formal process (what is written in the rule book or the bylaws), and that is one piece of what happens. How things actually get done may look very different.

One organizer told me that his group was pushing for the state legislature to enact a law that would keep predatory lending practices out of mortgages and mortgage refinances. His group lobbied the twelve members of the legislative committee but also exerted pressure on the Speaker of the House, a very influential man who had strong ties to a number of the committee members. "We met with him the night before and said, 'This is where folks are at. We expect you to make sure this happens.' We told him how far we had brought it and then laid it on him. We said, 'We know you have the power to make this happen.'" The bill made it through committee.

Utilize Networks to Effect Change

Community organizing efforts plumb the depths of all the networks represented by the people in your group. One of the values of working with a larger group of people is that each person has a circle of influence. Put all of those networks together, and you may be able to find a way to reach just about any decision maker in your geographic area, not to mention people who could help you with your campaign, such as members of the media.

Someone in your group may know someone who works in the mayor's office, helping you gain access to the mayor or knowledge about which issues are going to be considered by the city council and when. Someone else may have a contact in the police department, allowing you access to crime statistics that would otherwise be hard to get. And more than once people have told me about working with a local church pastor to influence change through an important decision maker who was a member of that pastor's church.

Taking Action

The ultimate end in a community organizing effort is to act, not just talk, research, write, or build relationships. All of those other efforts lead you toward collective action. Actions might include the following:

- Letter writing. People from your group write letters to the officials or leaders who can produce change, asking them to do something specific. The more letters the better. (See Model 4, pages 87–88.)
- Petitions. Another way to show the critical mass of support behind your issue is to collect signatures on a petition. Petitions are often delivered to officials or leaders at a public meeting.
- Boycotts. Boycott the goods or services of an organization to convince them to change.
- Use of the media. Build relationships with people in the media so that they will write stories about your efforts and show up to film key events. (See Model 4, page 89.)

- Picketing. Picket lines might be used to draw public attention to the issue, as well as to embarrass businesses or other organizations into action. One organizer told me about picketing two suburban gun shops that did a "dirty business" of selling guns to criminals—guns from the shops were linked to a number of crimes in city neighborhoods. The pickets attracted media attention, and a couple of reporters wrote stories that were instrumental in the gun shops being shut down.

- Hold meetings. Organizing groups often prep people to hold meetings. The agenda must be clear and focused with the primary audience in mind, so prepare well, develop an agenda, and identify one of your group members to run the meeting. Here are some types of meetings:

  □ Small group meetings with key decision makers. In this type of meeting, the focus is on making the case for your issue with a potential decision maker and presenting an "ask"—a request that the official do something specific.

  □ Large group meetings. This kind of meeting is an effort to "show your muscle" on an issue to elected officials or decision makers—if you can gather hundreds, perhaps even thousands of people, it demonstrates that you have a critical mass of people who care. These meetings usually have an agenda and often include the presence of public officials or other decision makers who listen to presentations by the group and answer questions from the crowd.

  □ Mass demonstrations such as marches or protests. In these very large meetings, you gather your coalition plus members of the broader public to march or protest around your issue. You may need to secure a permit for this type of meeting.

The Lasting Power of Organizing Skills

Learning how to organize can bring lasting change to your church in many areas, not just community ministry. Through the organizing process, church members can build relationships with one another that will help them work together in other ministry areas of the church and even work through conflict more effectively. Community organizing can also build skills in researching issues, leading meetings, and interacting with decision makers.

People in congregations that I spoke to about this model described with fondness the many people from other congregations and community groups they met and had gotten to know in a deep way. Working together on organizing projects, going through the ups and downs, being trained in techniques, and then working side by side can create bonds and skills that last far beyond a "win" on a particular issue.

What You'll Need

- Five to fifteen people from your congregation to help lead the process
- One or more issues that people in your congregation are passionate about
- Church members who are interested in building relationships with each other and with people in the community
- Training in one-on-one conversations and listening
- A ready-made coalition focused on organizing, or churches, nonprofits, businesses, and other organizations that want to pull together with your church to form a coalition
- A partner organization, like an affiliate of the Industrial Areas Foundation or the PICO National Network that can train church members in organizing techniques. This is not essential but is very helpful. If you join with a partner, you'll need money to pay dues to the organization.

MODEL 6

Develop a Ministry Program

WHAT IT IS: *Your church develops its own homegrown community ministry program, envisioned and planned by your leaders and members, and operated by them too. Your church dreams up the idea, puts together a plan, raises the resources, finds the people to staff the program, and then operates the program. This is different from having a partner organization offer programming on-site at your church (Model 3: "Partner with Other Organizations") or just leasing space within your church building to other organizations. This is your church hatching and nurturing a program that is your own.*

When God Calls Us to Structure the Work

The Hellenists complained against the Hebrews because their widows were being neglected in the daily distribution of food. And the twelve called together the whole community of the disciples and said, "It is not right that we should neglect the word of God in order to wait on tables. Therefore, friends, select from among yourselves seven men of good standing, full of the Spirit and of wisdom, whom we may appoint to this task."—ACTS 6:1-3

The disciples were clear about what they wanted to do. All widows were to be taken care of by the church, but the existing process was preventing this important task from being completed in an inclusive and just way. In this passage we get an interesting look inside the operations of the early church.

First, a need was identified—in this case, by people in the community who observed something that concerned them. They gave an eyewitness account of the neglect of certain widows—assessing a key issue for their community. Next, leaders acknowledged that a new way of doing business was needed—more structure must be brought to bear. They talked together about how best to respond, and the idea of finding seven members of the community who could take on this task was brought forward. They were looking for seven who were well known in the community of believers—seasoned people who had demonstrated their wisdom and spiritual maturity and who may have served the faith community in other capacities.

I can picture what probably happened next, though these steps are not detailed in the Scripture passage. The new program team (the seven) took on the task by planning further. Setting up a schedule for distribution may well have been one of the next steps. Also, identifying how supplies would be secured and who would do that must have been decided. They may well have worked to enlist other volunteers from their church community in their mission.

The disciples demonstrated the willingness to develop more structure when the work at hand required it. They are a witness to us in their humility, admitting that things weren't going so well! They model a willingness to listen to others and to let go of work that could clearly be done more effectively in another way. Developing a new program in a church often requires this level of humility and flexibility, and here we have a biblical model for how we might proceed when God calls us to greater structure.

An Exciting Process

Developing a new ministry program can be one of the most exciting processes in the life of a church. It is a time when vision and dreams are very present and when God can speak in new ways to the people in your church about serving the community.

One church caught the vision for providing affordable housing in a city neighborhood a short distance from their suburb. The pastor cast the initial vision for the program, but then volunteers from the church got involved, providing expertise (and muscle) to renovate the houses the church had purchased. The confirmation class got in on the action, helping with demolition. Talented decorators in the church helped make the housing units look bright and stylish.

When it was time for families to move in, volunteers from the church were trained as mentors, helping provide support and connecting families to resources. All the people I talked to at this church seemed to know about this program in some detail, either because they were involved themselves or because they knew someone who was. The program brought new spiritual life and energy to the church and helped members of this suburban congregation better understand the challenges faced by families in the city.

Just Be Sure

Even before identifying the challenges and advantages of this model, I must caution you: be *sure* before you choose to develop a new ministry program. Be sure that your new program is needed by the community and that it doesn't duplicate programs run by other organizations nearby. Be sure there is a match between your program idea and the gifts, skills, and passions within your congregation. Be sure you have enough capacity to offer the program and keep it going over a period of time.

Launching a program and ending it before it has even had a chance to develop can be devastating to the people in your church and really hard on the community. Laypeople (and staff) from your church who put time into developing the idea want to see the new program flourish. When it flops because you didn't plan well enough or lacked capacity to deliver the program, it will color how laypeople see other opportunities to serve (they might not be willing to). Also, community residents may develop a negative impression of your church and may not be willing to trust efforts that you make moving forward. So before you plan and launch a new program, be sure that it is the best model for your church.

Advantages of Developing Your Own Ministry Program

One of the best reasons to develop your own program is that you can tailor it to the gifts of your congregation. You are not trying to

fit your church members into someone else's dream; you are inviting them to come up with their own. Participate in the processes
outlined in "Meeting the Neighbors" and "Finding Your Congregation's Ministry Dream" in Part One.

Church members who are involved in the entire program design
process will feel more ownership of the idea and may be more willing to give their time and money as you implement the program.
And it is committed lay volunteers who keep a program going long
after the church staff member who was involved has moved on.

Programs that you design yourselves can also be tailored to meet
specific needs in the community (assuming you have identified those
needs by meeting the neighbors). If you see that a particular population of people is not being served well by other organizations, for
example, you can develop a program to serve them. You may have
new immigrants in your community who need culturally specific
programs that no one else provides, or middle-school students who
would not be served well by having to attend existing programs
tailored for younger children or high school students.

Alternatively, you may be working in a community where there
is a complete lack of certain kinds of services—maybe it is health
care for the uninsured. In that case, your church could fill the gap
by starting a community clinic, offering blood pressure or diabetes
screenings on a regular basis, or providing transportation to the
closest clinic, which may be a distance away.

Or your church may see a lack of programs with spiritual content, and that is what would make yours different. If you believe
that spiritual growth is critical to achieving your program outcomes, you may decide to develop a youth development program
with a clear Christian discipleship aspect, a transitional housing
program with Bible study and prayer built in, or a support group
for people in addiction recovery that has a clear focus on a relationship with Jesus Christ.

Challenges of Developing Your Own Ministry Program

As implied in the caution above, one of the challenges of this model
is that you really do need a certain level of capacity within your
church to develop and run your own program. I work with congregations on a regular basis that are strong on the vision part but not

so great on the implementation. You can see that your neighborhood really needs an after-school tutoring program, for example, and where you might hold it and which kids could come. If the rest seems a little fuzzy, you should push yourself toward a program design process (described later in this chapter) to see if you can identify more of the specifics and to assess whether you have the capacity to deliver the program.

This model typically takes more resources to operate than the previous models described in this book, and that may be challenging for some congregations. Most programs require space to operate, supplies and equipment, and a significant amount of people power. If you need paid staff to run the program, you'll need to ask one or more church staff members to get involved or raise money for a paid staff position. Using volunteers may be an option, but they will need to be recruited, trained, and supervised. Before seriously considering this model, take stock of all the resources you will need and assess your congregation's ability to secure them.

Another resource you will need is expertise in the program field you have decided to work in. In fact, you ought to choose your program focus based, in part, on whether you have some experts in the field "nearby" (in the congregation or community) who can help you design the program. If your dream is to start a health-focused program, are there people from the health field in your congregation or community who can advise you on how to do that? Doctors or nurses could be helpful, also health educators, dieticians, physical therapists, psychologists, and many other types of health professionals. A partner organization could also help provide expertise as you are designing your program, but that will require a hybrid approach (see pages 157–158).

This model also carries the danger of duplicating what has already been done in your community. In my experience, some churches jump too quickly to develop their own programs before doing a thorough scan of the community to see what else is out there. If there is already an agency nearby providing senior services, for example, ask yourselves some hard questions about why you think you need to start from scratch and develop your own chore service or visiting nurse program. You may ultimately decide that a partnership developed under Model 3 may be just as effective and potentially more beneficial.

It may also be that developing your own ministry program has some downsides compared to creating a nonprofit (see Model 7). Working within the structure of the church means that the idea for your new program will have to fit in the church budget, share space within the church building (unless you decide to offer your program off-site), fit into the overall church program schedule, receive approval from church leaders, and share fund-raising and volunteer recruitment time with other programs in the church. Often, churches start nonprofits because it is taking too long to develop a program idea under the church—program ideas are put into a queue together to wait for church resources to be made available.

The Dignity Center: Building Program Infrastructure as the Program Grows

The Dignity Center is a program of Hennepin Avenue United Methodist Church, located on the edge of downtown Minneapolis. At the time the program was founded, the need for it was obvious to anyone who came into or out of the church on a weekday. Homeless people who had no place else to go during the day were walking through the neighborhood or camped out on sidewalks. This was the case at any time of the year, even during the coldest months.

In the years since it was founded, the Dignity Center has turned many corners, developing new infrastructure and program elements as the vision for the program and the needs of the people being served became clearer. At first the program served more as a day center for the homeless, where they could come to get food, clothing, and other basic needs items. But the center has evolved into a program that promotes self-sufficiency and stability, focusing most of its resources on clients who are pursuing education and making progress on goals.

The Dignity Center provides a good example of what needs to happen in many community ministry programs. Hitting obstacles or challenges often doesn't mean it is time to give up; more often it means it is time to rethink the elements of the program, who is involved, what is expected of participants, and strategies for finding resources.

As the program grew over the years, more infrastructure was added to make it sustainable. The program was started with a couple of paid staff, but a shift was made to attract and train more volunteers. Program leaders found they could serve more people and provide more services by significantly expanding the number of volunteers involved. Volunteer job descriptions were developed with a clear differentiation in duties between the types of volunteers. A structured training program was developed that includes a shadowing program—new volunteers follow a seasoned one for six weeks to learn how to conduct client interviews, use the referral notebook, and understand the criteria for distributing physical resources such as food.

Volunteer participation has grown from five people at the founding of the program to eighty people today, with volunteers fulfilling a variety of roles. Ann Carlson, director of the Dignity Center, says, "When you do a large ministry, you need many kinds of volunteers. Not everyone wants to work directly with clients, but we have someone who fixes our donated computers, a graphic designer who puts together our pamphlets, and someone else who copies them and sends them out. Another of our volunteers does our end-of-month statistics and purchases food and puts it away."

Another way new infrastructure was built was by creating an intake form so volunteers could develop a file on clients from the outset, with a clear documentation of goals, needs, and resources that clients already had. The leadership also developed focus areas for the program so volunteers could help participants develop and work toward clear goals—for example, in jobs, education, and health.

As the focus of the program changed, the Dignity Center changed the items they gave out to clients. The center used to give underwear and socks, but they discovered that many programs serving the homeless did that. As the focus shifted to help participants get into school and training programs, the center began to give out office and school supplies instead. Now participants can get folders, notebooks, appointment calendars, and even a refurbished computer if they are making strong progress on their goals.

As the program grew, new church partners were added. Over time it became clear that Hennepin Avenue Church couldn't sustain the program on its own. So new partner churches were recruited. Some churches were only ready to provide sandwiches and cookies, so they did that. Other congregations were able to provide volunteers to serve as advocates and in other roles.

Just this year, more changes were made. A new "cloud-based" database was purchased that can generate many types of preset reports that track the progress of clients. Every advocate who works with participants has access to an iPad, allowing them to scan case notes and referral sources.

Forming Your Program Development Team

Getting lay leaders involved at the beginning of new program development can lead to more enthusiasm for the program within the congregation because you are creating "champions" who can talk up the idea and enlist support for it.

Form a program development team that will "catch" new ideas and clarify program outcomes, develop a program plan including timelines, prepare a budget and funding strategy for the program, and identify staff and volunteer roles for the program. Your program development team will differ from other core volunteer groups at the church because it is solely focused on the feasibility of this new ministry idea without having to deal with competing agendas from other groups in the church.

There is great power in engaging church members from the start of new program development—it is giving them the packet of seeds and the plot of ground, rather than simply inviting them to help you tend plants that are already growing.

Consider forming a team that includes the following:

- A majority of people with passion for the idea
- Team membership that spans the generations, especially if your program will serve a particular age range. Be sure to include plenty of youth if youth programs are your goal, seniors for senior programs, and so on.
- At least a few church members who live in the community your program is designed to serve. They can provide invaluable "ground-level" insight and introduce you to neighbors who are potential partners and resources.
- One or two key leaders from within the congregation: members of the church board or council, for example, or heads of key ministry areas that have some connection to

the new program idea. So if you are developing an after-school program for children, consider involving current leaders in the children's ministry at your church. Having leadership support will help you along the way as you may need to ask for space in the church, staff time, funding, or other resources.

- People with expertise in fields related to the new program: educators for education programs, property development people for housing programs, and so on.

Developing Program Outcomes

Program development starts here: through your program outcomes you articulate what you hope will change in the world as a result of your program. These are your hoped-for results—not just a list of activities you offer or the number of people served. Instead, you ask, at the end of the day, how will the people who participate in this program be different? Will they have jobs? Will they have graduated from high school? Will they have lost weight because of healthy eating and exercise choices?

"Measuring Success in Your Ministry" in Part Three details the process of setting and measuring outcomes.

Designing a Program from Scratch

Once your program development team is in place and you have developed a couple of key program outcomes, your team can work together to develop an overall design for the program, a plan that identifies the program's specific elements. People outside your church ought to be able to read this document and get a picture of what you will be offering. They should be able to understand the who, where, what, and with whom of the program.

Elements of a Program Design

Key program outcomes. What are one or two key outcomes for program participants? How, specifically, will their lives change because they participate in your program? (See pages 159–166.)

Target audience. Who is being served by the program? Get as specific here as you can. Your target audience will inform your program design as you tailor your program to the specific needs of the group you have identified. For instance, youth development programs vary greatly depending on the age of the youth being served—teens are interested in different activities than five-year-olds. Here are some examples of target audiences:

- Children in grades three through six who attend the local public elementary school
- Families without health insurance who live in the north and central neighborhoods
- Homeless young adults ages eighteen to twenty-four who are currently living in a shelter
- Senior citizens over age seventy-five who are still living in their homes

Program content. This section of a program design document describes the content and activities you will deliver to your target audience. What exactly is being offered? Here are three ways you could describe the content of your ministry program:

- *Services provided.* These might include training and mentoring in how to apply for a job, after-school tutoring in reading and math skills, or cooking classes focused on healthy eating.
- *Session activities.* Here you get more specific. Try to give a visual of what participants would do while they are participating in your program:
  □ A six-week cooking class that meets in the church kitchen two consecutive nights each week. During the first weekly session, participants will learn about balanced and healthy eating from an instructor, construct a menu, and go to the grocery store to purchase ingredients. The following evening, participants will prepare the meal and eat it together.
  □ The bike shop operated by the church offers on-the-job youth employment skills training. Youth receive three hours of training each week on bike repair, customer service techniques, and business management and work five hours each week in the store.

- *Sequence of activities (over time).* There is often a "sequence" to services—starting with the basics and then working on more complex goals as the program participants develop more skill or independence. For example, many groups that serve the homeless provide case management services to clients over a period of time. If living more independently is the goal down at the "finish line" for your participants, then the "flow" of your services might be:
  1. Provide housing (getting the person off the street).
  2. Meet other basic needs (food and clothing).
  3. Help the participant set goals for independence.
  4. Connect them to physical and mental health resources.
  5. Get them connected to a GED (graduate equivalency diploma) program, job training, or college classes.
  6. Work on gaining employment or better employment.

Frequency. Describe when and how often the program will be held. How many days a week or times per month? How many hours at a time? At what time of day? For example, on Tuesdays of every week from 2:00 to 4:00 p.m.

Location. Identify the location where the program will be held. Think about the kind of space (or spaces) you will need to operate the program. Is there enough room for the number of participants you anticipate will attend? What kind of space will you need? Do you need space for quiet activities (like reading or homework) or for more active activities (aerobics class or dodge ball)? Does the space need to be private for confidential activities like counseling, as well as accessible to people with disabilities? What security procedures will you need, and would the space be safe for young children? Access to public transportation may be important as well. Also consider how custodial support will be provided. And make sure the space is actually available when you need it—check the schedule of activities on an ongoing basis!

Supplies and equipment needed. Identify the materials you will need for your program and how you will secure them. Visualize your program in operation and walk through the supplies and equipment you will need so that you can have everything ready before you begin. You don't want to be in the middle of a program session and realize you forgot to bring the _____ (you fill in the blank—pencils, baseballs, hammers, blood pressure cuffs, snacks, etc.).

Partner organizations. If applicable, which groups will you partner with to offer the program? You may decide to collaborate with another organization to provide an element of your program. Is there something that your participants need that your church can't provide but that another nearby group could? Maybe the local bank could send over staff to teach personal financial management to your participants. Or perhaps the health clinic nearby could provide education on exercise and nutrition to youth. Churches with a vision to build affordable housing often partner with another organization with expertise in property development and financing. Look for groups that can add value to what you are able to deliver. Model 3 includes tips on how to choose a partner.

Human resources. How many and what types of volunteers will you need for the program? Will the program require the commitment of paid staff to get it started or keep it going? If so, will you need part-time or full-time workers? Many new community ministry programs depend on volunteers to implement them and hire paid staff later as the program "gains steam." Model 2 provides detailed instructions on what you will need to put in place to recruit and prepare your volunteers.

If you decide you do need paid staff from the start of your program, you will need to do the following:

- Define the responsibilities you need to be fulfilled by paid staff. Will staff be responsible for creating the program from the ground up or for implementation only? Do you need on-site staff to be in an oversight or supervisory role, or will they serve more in administrative capacities (filing reports, writing correspondence, maintaining a database, etc.)?
- Identify to whom the staff persons will report. Will they be part of any existing teams at the church? To which lay leader, church staff member, or committee will they be accountable?
- Develop a job description for each paid position that includes duties, qualifications, desired traits, and experiences.
- Develop a plan for hiring paid staff. How will you get the word out? Which people or networks will you ask to promote/advertise the position? Who will conduct the interview process and make the hire?

Program budget. Your program budget should include expenses like program staff salaries and benefits, supplies and equipment, transportation, copying and postage, and food. But don't forget to include less obvious "overhead" expenses like the cost of the space used by the program and a portion of the cost of liability insurance.

Financial resources. Most programs need some level of financial support to be launched, even if it is just a little bit of money for supplies. Putting together your program budget will help you know how much money you need. Depending on the type of program you are seeking to get funded, support may come from other churches, individual donors (including people in your church), foundation and corporate grant funders, government sources, service clubs and fraternities, or denominational grants. "Securing Funds for Your Ministry" in Part Three provides detailed information on how to seek grants, donations from individuals, and other types of funding.

Putting It All Together: Program Design at a Glances:

- Key program outcomes
- Target audience
- Program content
- Frequency
- Location
- Supplies and equipment needed
- Partner organizations
- Human resources
- Program budget
- Financial resources

Evaluate and Tweak

No program is perfect, and you will discover this as you move to implement your program design. Inevitably, you will find that something didn't quite turn out as you expected and you will need to "tweak" the program, adjusting the content to better meet participant needs or moving the program to a new location to make it more accessible to your target audience. Over the years, programs I have worked with have had to, among other things, change operating hours, buy more food, add a sports component to the curriculum, train more volunteers, start providing transportation, and communicate more effectively with their partner organization. Tweaking is a natural part of program development, and evaluating your work continuously will help you know where you need to make changes. Always ask these questions:

- Were the overall outcomes of the program achieved?
- Were participants satisfied with the program?
- What was the experience like for our volunteers?
- What do our partner organizations say about the program?

Returning to these questions on a regular basis will help you continuously improve your ministry program. And that will be good for your church *and* your community.

What You'll Need

Here is a list of what is helpful to have in place at your church if you are looking to develop your own ministry program.

EARLY ON

- A small group of church volunteers with a vision for the program and a passion to see it developed
- A strong sense of what the community wants and needs (see Part One, pages 11–17)
- Information on what is being offered by other groups in the community. What are the gaps in services?
- Clarity on the gifts, interests, and passions present in your congregation (see Part One: "Finding Your Congregation's Ministry Dream")
- One or two key program outcomes—how will people's lives change as a result of participating in your program?

THEN

- At least one church staff person who can devote time to overseeing the program development process

- A design for the program. Who is being served? What, specifically, is being offered? When and where is it offered?

ON IMPLEMENTATION

- Space (and the right kind of it) where the program can be offered
- The necessary equipment and supplies
- The ability to staff the program with either paid staff or unpaid volunteers
- Funds to cover program expenses, including staff, supplies, food, transportation, publicity, events, and so on

MODEL 7

Create a Church-Based Nonprofit*

WHAT IT IS: *Establishing a separate 501(c)3 nonprofit organization that is connected to the congregation in some way, either through its governance structure, shared programs, staff and other resources, or partnerships.* Usually a nonprofit is established to house one or more existing community ministry programs once the programs have become too large or too complex for the congregation to sustain on its own. Some churches with a large number of community ministry programs might decide to form more than one nonprofit—one nonprofit that is a school, one for a health clinic, and so on.*

See, I Am Doing a New Thing

"I am about to do a new thing; now it springs forth, do you not perceive it?"
—ISAIAH 43:19

The desire to start a new organization often starts with new thinking—the desire to make a new and better way to serve the community and/or wanting to create new ways to engage the church. While there are certainly administrative and legal details involved,

*In the interest of space, I have not included a description of the legal process of forming a nonprofit organization in this chapter.

the process of creating a new nonprofit organization is more like planning for a pregnancy or planting a garden. It is far more than filling out the right paperwork. People who start church-based non-profits often come first with a vision—of what is possible, of what the new thing looks like. In my experience, those visions often come from God; they are evidence of God doing a new thing.

To really consider a new structure, like starting a new nonprofit, a congregation needs to be open to the new thing God is doing, and with that comes risks. You will need to see ministry in a new way, look at your congregation in a new way, and look at your community differently too. The passage in Isaiah asks, "Do you not perceive it?" Part of your prayer should be for eyes to see the new thing God is doing in your midst.

When Is It Time to Consider Starting a Nonprofit?

People often ask me, "When will I know it's time to start a nonprofit at our church?" My first recommendation is to start your nonprofit after you have some ministry programs to put in it. You won't know if you need a whole other organization to sustain and grow your ministries if you don't have any ministries yet! The picture differs from congregation to congregation, but generally I say that the best time to move forward is when your community ministry programs want to burst forward to the next level to grow in size or complexity and being in the church structure holds them back. Maybe your church lacks the financial resources or volunteers needed to help your community ministry grow. A separate nonprofit could help your programs expand to the next level.

For example, say your church starts an after-school program two days a week. Over time it grows to four days a week and the number of children served quadruples. You soon realize that dedi-cated staff members need to be hired to run the program, and the church cannot finance this on its own. Also, you need to move the program to a new, nearby location because the program has out-grown the space at the church. You need funding from foundations that will not give directly to a church; also, you need to partner with one or more groups (including the local school) that will be more willing to connect with an organization that is not a church congregation.

You will want to pull together a team of staff and lay leaders to serve as the steering committee for the nonprofit. This group will consider whether to form a nonprofit in the first place, and if the answer is yes, they will provide leadership through the process of developing a plan, determining the connection between the two organizations, forming a board, and completing the legal process.

Don't Start a Nonprofit If . . .

It is tempting to start a nonprofit for the following reasons, but don't. It is your ministry dream that should drive this decision, not pursuing the formation of the nonprofit.

- Don't do it just to get the money. Being able to access new sources of funds is a reason to start a nonprofit but shouldn't be the primary motivating factor.
- Don't do it just because everyone else is doing it. Don't develop a new organization just because all of the other churches in your denomination are doing it or because this is what you need to do to seem "relevant," big enough, or influential.
- Don't do it just because one or two people in your church want to do it. Forming a nonprofit is a large group effort, requiring the goodwill of the congregation as a whole and a number of "workers" to step forward.

Advantages of Creating a Church-Based Nonprofit

The main reason churches start nonprofits is to tap into funding sources that wouldn't (or couldn't) support a church. Many foundations, corporations, and even individuals and other churches may feel uncomfortable giving directly to a church congregation. Some corporations and foundations even have a clause in their bylaws or guidelines specifying that they can't give directly to "sectarian" organizations because their vision is to serve the entire community, not just one religious group within it. Setting up a separate 501(c)3 nonprofit with its own set of books, funding streams, and distinct programs creates a separation from the church that may make it possible for these funders to support your work.

Having a nonprofit may also enhance your ability to collaborate with "secular" organizations in your community. Sometimes the spiritual nature of a congregation is a barrier for "secular" groups—they may think they can't work with you if they aren't Methodist or Presbyterian or Christian like you are. Another barrier is that some people automatically assume that the underlying purpose of the church and all of its efforts is to recruit new members. Approaching a potential partner as the nonprofit may help remove that suspicion. So in seeking partners to work against gun violence, for example, you could say to the police department, public schools, county social services, local youth center, neighborhood associations, parent groups, public health agency, and other churches and faith communities, "We want your help on our gun violence project, regardless of whether you share our spiritual beliefs or not."

Having a nonprofit may also help you enlist a greater variety and number of volunteers than you would as a church. This could be critical to the success of your programs if your own congregation can't provide enough people with the right skills. It could be there are people in your community who would never volunteer at your church because they aren't Christian, aren't churchgoers, or go to another church. But if you asked them to volunteer for your youth development nonprofit as homework helpers, they might just say yes.

Another advantage of having a nonprofit organization is that it might be able to make decisions more quickly than a church congregation, which will be important to you if you need to respond quickly to ministry opportunities that arise. Nonprofits can often be nimbler than churches in bringing new programs into being and securing the resources for them. Not all churches are slow-moving, but in my experience, many are. By the time an idea has passed through church committees, been approved by the church board and voted on by the congregation, the grant deadline has passed or the property has been sold, and you may have missed out on something that could have moved your vision forward.

Establishing a nonprofit is also a way to "institutionalize" your community ministry program, a signal both to your church members and the community that you are in it for the long haul. Having an independent organization helps you keep programs going even when the original group of founders or volunteers moves on.

Challenges of Creating a Church-Based Nonprofit

Starting and managing a nonprofit does require administrative ability—and not all congregations possess this. If your church has a hard time keeping schedules, developing plans, following through on details, and completing necessary paperwork, this may not be the right model for you. Sometimes I have people in my "Starting a Nonprofit at Your Church" class who conclude that they want to spend their time focused on direct ministry, not running an organization. That said, it may also be possible to add staff to handle administrative matters or to recruit volunteers (perhaps from outside your church) who bring administrative expertise.

This model also increases the chance that your community ministry will drift from its faith focus, particularly if you set up the organization to have very little structural connection to the congregation. You probably wouldn't have to look very far in your own community to find a now-secular nonprofit that started out connected to a church.

Consider this example: A church starts a transitional housing program with a strong faith focus, with clients participating in Bible study, prayer time, and discipleship activities every week. But when more and more people from outside the church are added to the nonprofit board, they begin to question the faith aspect of the program. Perhaps your nonprofit secures more and more funding from "secular" foundations (ones without a spiritual focus or interest) and you become accustomed to separating out the spiritual activities, viewing them as less important or optional. When this kind of funding becomes a large portion of the support for the nonprofit, it becomes difficult not to listen to the wishes of the funders. It is not a given that this "faith drift" will occur, but forming a separate organization creates at least somewhat of a barrier between the church and the nonprofit.

A related challenge is that nonprofits and the churches that create them can grow apart. What once was ministry synergy can become at best a lack of alignment and, at worst, full-blown conflict about which ministries are pursued, how they are operated, who gets to do what, even administrative details. My family once attended a church where many church members strongly disagreed with how the church's nonprofit interacted with the community.

New ministries were developed without the input of neighborhood residents, and as a result, those ministries were controversial in the community. This led to factions being formed in the church—one group thought the nonprofit was doing great work; the other group had concerns. One conflict was about the nonprofit buying up property to convert into ministry sites. Neighbors wanted to retain these locations as housing and keep them on the property tax rolls.

Another challenge—you will have to raise money. Having a nonprofit costs more than not having one, even if your nonprofit runs largely on volunteer labor. You will have filing fees to acquire and keep your nonprofit status plus liability insurance costs. And if you decide to hire staff, you will have salaries to pay plus benefits and staff training costs. So if fund-raising is not your deal, your church may want to select another model. However, if you are willing to fund-raise but just don't know how, you can learn (see "Securing Funds for Your Ministry" in Part Three).

One final note: This is a difficult model to pull off if your church is in transition or facing great difficulties. It may not be the right time to form a nonprofit if the church is in the midst of a pastoral search, a capital campaign, or some kind of relational conflict. Giving birth to a nonprofit requires an ability to come together that may be difficult if you are divided about something else.

RiverWorks: A Church-Based Nonprofit "Owned" by the Whole Town

RiverWorks is a nonprofit that was founded by Riverwood Covenant Church in Rockford, a town in central Minnesota. The vision for the nonprofit came from a layperson in the church who saw that the congregation had great potential for developing new programs to meet community needs but didn't have all of the resources needed to realize the vision on its own. "We all saw that this was bigger than what our church itself could handle—we really needed to form a 501(c)3 nonprofit," said Denise Kesanen, RiverWorks director.

The initial vision of the nonprofit to offer tutoring and a home nursing service shifted as community research was done. It turned out that tutoring wasn't needed as much as was initially thought—another group in town had started to provide it. And there just didn't seem to be enough energy among potential volunteers to begin a nursing program. But staff and church members had begun to hear from more and more people in town that a food shelf was needed.

Operators of the food shelf in the next town said they were overwhelmed by the needs in the community and that many current clients were coming from Rockford. RiverWorks formed a community-wide task force to discuss how a food shelf could be launched in their town. When the resources seemed to fall into place (volunteers stepped to the plate, and the city donated use of a building for the program), the food shelf at RiverWorks was launched.

Other programs have been developed since, usually arising out of conversations with people in the broader community. For example, a thrift store provides low-cost clothing and household goods to the community while raising money for RiverWorks projects.

The nonprofit has developed a business model that starts with events that build awareness. Then they develop programs from the relationships formed at the events. An annual steak fry, for example, and the Roundup (dinner at a ranch, horseback riding, and Old West activities) have helped raise the visibility of the nonprofit and have also provided the opportunity to hear from community residents about their needs and dreams.

"The people of our town are so behind what we are doing," said Kesanen. "The events have made a big difference in this—people know who we are and what we are doing, and they get a sense of how they can join in. It has been neat to see people from all walks of life attend the events, people who don't normally interact with each other." Kesanen said that the RiverWorks logo is prominently displayed on the outside of City Hall, right below the WELCOME TO ROCKFORD sign and right next to the Lions Club logo and the City Government seal. The strong support of the town is evident in the many contributions that residents make toward the work of River-Works, giving their money, their time, and their material goods to a work they believe in.

The RICC in New Orleans: Planting a Church and a Nonprofit at the Same Time

The Restoration Initiative for Culture and Community (the RICC) in New Orleans is a new church-based nonprofit connected to Canal Street Church: A Mosaic Community, an Evangelical Covenant

Church plant. Forming both organizations at the same time is helping to ensure that "community restoration is part of the heartbeat of our church," said Michael Hitch, director of the RICC. "So many people and communities in New Orleans are open to restoration activity since Katrina—on all levels—that we wanted to create a way for the church to partner with others to engage in community development work."

The new nonprofit is building on the assets of people in the church by starting with arts programming for youth. (There are many musicians and visual artists in the church.) A leadership academy for middle and high school youth will begin soon and will include a counseling component and fine arts programming. A monthly "café" is also being developed, using the industrial kitchen in the church building. This is envisioned as a place where artists can come to create and perform work on a different theme each month—themes such as racial reconciliation and justice. "We wanted to create a space in our city where people can come into a faith context and discuss hard issues," said Hitch. The hope is that the café will develop into a culinary arts training program with the help of an executive chef from the church.

While plans were being developed for the leadership academy and the café, Hurricane Isaac struck, drawing the church and nonprofit into relief work. "This was never a part of our vision for the nonprofit, but it was an immediate need that required attention," Hitch said. Staff of the nonprofit are putting together a disaster relief "toolbox" for other nonprofits, recognizing that the people of New Orleans have developed a core competency in this area over the years because of their experience responding to the aftermath of storms.

Forming a Board of Directors

All 501(c)3 nonprofit organizations are required by law to have a board of directors. The minimum number of people required to serve on a board varies state by state. The board is the highest authority within a nonprofit and has authority to make decisions about the finances and staffing of the organization, its strategic direction, and programs. The board of directors is not just advisory in nature—it is responsible for governing the entire nonprofit. If your nonprofit has an executive director, the board has the authority to hire and fire that person.

The Role of the Board

How involved the board will get in the details and day-to-day operations of the nonprofit is an important decision to make as your nonprofit is being formed. A tactical board (my phrase; also called a working board) is much more involved in running the actual organization. Board members might run programs, recruit and train volunteers, staff the office, and write grants, for example. Many new organizations start with a tactical board and move to a board that is more "navigational" in nature as staff are added. As the organization grows and staff members take on more of the day-to-day operational responsibilities, the board becomes more focused on the "big picture."

A navigational board (again my phrase; also called an oversight board) leaves the day-to-day operations to the staff and focuses on "big picture" issues only, such as setting the mission and vision of the organization and working with key staff to develop a strategic plan for the organization, establishing policies for human resources and financial management (among many other areas of the organization), and supervising and evaluating the executive director or other chief staff member of the nonprofit (but probably not other nonprofit staff).

Often tension within a board begins with a lack of clarity about what type of board the organization has or needs. Sometimes board members meddle in the details of the organization when staff members just want to be left alone to do their jobs. But sometimes a board needs to be much more hands-on yet won't engage, leaving key tasks undone.

Usually a shift in the role of the board is from tactical to navigational when the organization grows and adds staff members who take over the day-to-day operational duties. However, in times of economic distress or change when organizations need to downsize, boards may need to shift from a navigational role to performing more hands-on tasks, particularly if some of the staff have been let go. Making these shifts is what I like to call "turning the corner with the board." It is always hard and, in my experience, requires really honest conversation.

If you are experiencing tension within your board, it may be time to pause, take some time together to review the roles and expectations of the board, and identify what type of board the organization needs going forward. I find that board members are often relieved to have this conversation. They want to help the organization but don't know what to do. Or they feel the tension and don't know how to resolve it.

Sample Job Description for a Nonprofit Board of Directors

(Note: This job description is most appropriate for a navigational board.)

Spiritual leadership. Perform duties in a manner consistent with the spiritual principles of the organization. [Specific beliefs could be articulated here or could be left out for nonprofits that do not have a spiritual focus or for those that intend to have an interfaith board.]

Strategic planning. Oversee strategic planning efforts for the nonprofit. Review strategic plan annually to check the organization's progress against the goals.

Evaluation. Ensure that all programs and staff are evaluated at least annually. Review evaluation reports to identify areas for improvement and oversee development of plan to address these issues.

Financial oversight. Approve annual budget and review any significant changes made to the budget during the year. Monitor cash flow and ensure that an audit of the organization's finances is conducted annually.

Legal issues. Ensure that the organization is in compliance with all relevant laws and regulations. Ensure that there are adequate risk management procedures, including the purchase of necessary liability insurance.

Personnel issues. Hire, supervise, and evaluate the executive director. Develop and approve personnel policies for the organization.

Communications and promotions. Ensure that the organization has a communications plan. Promote the organization whenever possible through business and personal contacts.

Resource development. Ensure that the organization has adequate resources for its programs and operations. Raise funds for the organization from foundation, corporate, and individual sources. Plan and implement special fund-raising events.

Board development. Monitor the work of the board on a regular basis and put processes in place to recruit new board members.

Governance Models for a Church-Based Nonprofit

Forming a board is an important step for a nonprofit, but you will also need to make a few other key decisions about your board model as you set up the nonprofit. Some of these relate to how the governance of the nonprofit is connected to the church. Three board models for church-based nonprofits can be downloaded at the Judson Press website at judsonpress.com/downloads.

You will need to make these key decisions when developing your board model:

■ *Will the nonprofit have its own separate board of directors, or will it be governed by the leadership board of the church?* (Your congregation may call it the vestry, council, session, executive council, etc.) An upside of placing the church board in this role is that the nonprofit will remain very tied to the church. Also, it is a great way to get started if you want to move your nonprofit forward quickly, without taking the time to form a separate board. A downside of having your church board play this dual role is that they may not have time to adequately oversee the nonprofit. Also, you won't have the option of selecting board members from outside your congregation—a real downside if you need outside people with particular expertise and connections to help move the nonprofit forward. A separate board for the nonprofit gives you at least some freedom to recruit the board members you want and need (rather than having to "make do" with whoever is on the church board).

■ *Will there be a requirement that some of the board members of the nonprofit also be members of the church?* One way to maintain a tie between the nonprofit and the church is to require that a certain number or percentage of the nonprofit's board be members of the church. For greater ownership by and accountability to the church, you may want to require that a majority of nonprofit board members be church members. To simply ensure that the church's voice and interests are represented, require a smaller percentage or even just one or two church members. Including church members on the nonprofit board may not be a concern for your church—

some congregations form nonprofits without any ongoing tie to the church at all.

■ *Will the church leadership board have the right of "secondary approval" for any of the nonprofit board's decisions?* Talk about whether the church board will sign off on the nonprofit's strategic plan, budget, or hiring decisions, for example.

Questions of Control and Connection

What is the connection between the church and the nonprofit? And how much control will the church want to have over the new organization? These are important questions to ask at the very beginning of the process of forming a nonprofit. Finding the answers will help you to select a board model. This can be a difficult conversation. All parties need to discuss openly their expectations for how the new organization will interface with the church, connect with its ministries, and help the congregation prosper. You want to avoid a situation down the road where church leaders expected to have a great deal of say over the direction and operation of the nonprofit but the nonprofit leaders understood that they had free rein over the organization.

The church could choose to have a great deal of control over the nonprofit or choose to grant the nonprofit independence, allowing the staff and board of the nonprofit to make their own decisions. In my own experience, church-based nonprofits seem to work best when the nonprofit retains some connection to the church—being able to recruit volunteers from the church, utilize church members' expertise, or rely on them for financial support. Other areas where the church can undergird the nonprofit (particularly as the organization gets started) include involving the pastor and other church staff and lay leaders, providing administrative support, and helping develop marketing strategies. However, when churches hold on to their nonprofits too tightly, that defeats the purpose of starting a separate organization. When the same people and structures are involved, there may be very little added value to incorporating a 501(c)3. When church leaders are willing to give the nonprofit at least some autonomy, the new organization can more successfully reach out of the church toward potential funders and partners.

These are some areas of the new nonprofit where the church may want to exercise some control:

Role of the pastor. How will the pastor of the church be engaged with the nonprofit? Will the pastor supervise any of the nonprofit's staff? Will the pastor sit on the nonprofit's board?

Human resource management. Who hires the director of the nonprofit and other nonprofit staff? Who supervises the director—the board of the nonprofit or the pastor of the church? Are the hiring standards for nonprofit staff the same as for church staff—or different? What lifestyle and theological beliefs might nonprofit staff be expected to adhere to (as church staff are)? Who is responsible for evaluating staff and dealing with performance/discipline issues?

Selection of board members. Who recruits board members for the nonprofit? Who approves the slate of board members?

Making financial decisions. Who approves the annual budget for the nonprofit and reviews financial reports on a regular basis? Who approves major expenditures and the annual audit? Who develops financial policies for the nonprofit— where funds can be invested, for example? Who is liable for errors in financial records or misuse of funds? What about property acquisition or capital spending? What role (if any) do denominational staff have in such decisions?

Fund-raising. Who is responsible for raising funds for the nonprofit? Who approves any major fund-raising campaigns?

Mission and vision of the nonprofit. Who develops the mission and vision statements for the nonprofit? Who is authorized or empowered to revise that mission or vision as the ministry matures and evolves?

Strategic planning for the nonprofit. Who develops and approves the strategic direction for the organization, including priorities for the coming year and action plans for implementing them?

New programs or collaborative partnerships. Who approves new programs that the nonprofit would like to undertake, as well as major, new collaborative partnerships?

A Recruiting Process for Forming Your Board

Some nonprofits aren't very intentional about who ends up on the board, just pulling in who is nearby or whoever seems like they might be good. This haphazard and opportunistic approach rarely works. You can end up with board members who aren't clear about what is expected of them and who may not be very motivated to serve the organization well. I can't tell you how many board recruiting processes I have been involved in that try to start like this (and I usually try to help them head in a different direction): "We need a lawyer, an accountant, that corporate bigwig, and a politician— that's it!" All of these people may be talented, capable people, but they may not be who you need to get your nonprofit going.

Develop an intentional recruiting process to get the board you want. This involves identifying a larger pool of potential candidates and intentionally whittling down the list to fit what the nonprofit needs. Develop a clear job description for your board members (see "Sample Job Description for a Nonprofit Board of Directors" on page 133) that identifies their key roles and tasks. Then form a group of people to brainstorm potential candidates based on the needs identified in the board job description. Your group members should then meet one-on-one with potential candidates to discuss the possibility of their serving on the board (but not inviting them to serve). Finally, the group will need to reconvene to narrow down your list to the best candidates.

Many nonprofits provide board members with training each year on the duties and role of the board, the legal responsibilities of boards, and board-staff relationships. Training can also include discussion and planning of the key tasks the board will work to accomplish in the coming year.

A Commitment to Strong Church-Nonprofit Communication

More often than not, the relationship between a church and its nonprofit "child" breaks down because of poor communication between the two organizations. Without good communication, you might find that people in the other group misunderstand what you are trying to do, or that they have some information or connection that would have helped you get your work done. Sometimes information needs to be shared in order to coordinate or schedule church and nonprofit programs or events.

For example, if the nonprofit plans to do a big volunteer recruitment push in a Sunday church service, asking church members to participate in its local school partnership, this would need to be coordinated with the church's efforts to recruit volunteers for VBS. Maybe the nonprofit would want to avoid the Sunday when the church ministry is recruiting volunteers, or maybe the two organizations could coordinate their efforts, presenting to the congregation a united front and several options for volunteering. Below are some other areas of work for both organizations that may need coordination. You'll only find out about these by communicating.

- Scheduling use of space at the church building
- Planning major events that involve church members
- Asking church members for money (very important to coordinate! I have seen nonprofits severely damage the relationship with their mother church by doing "off the cuff" fund-raising solicitations of church members.)
- Launching of a major new program

A commitment to good communication means that nonprofit and church leaders will need to have "face time" with each other on a regular basis just to talk together about what is happening in each organization and how that might impact the other. Connecting with each other is particularly important when one or both organizations are pursuing something complex or multifaceted, when one organization is going through a great deal of change (a major staff transition, for example), or when tension already exists between leaders of the two groups. Following are some strategies for connecting face-to-face:

- Have combined staff meetings, if not every week, then perhaps monthly or quarterly.
- Schedule regular meetings of the nonprofit director and the church pastor.

- Hold concurrent board meetings, where at least one session involves boards of both organizations.
- Plan regular joint meetings for the boards of both organizations.
- Send key leaders from both organizations on an annual planning retreat. It can be helpful to get off-site and talk to each other about your plans and dreams for the coming year, and see what synergy might develop!
- Schedule regular fellowship opportunities for staff or board members of both groups (for example, a workday lunch, social outing, or family picnic). Doing something social allows everyone to get to know one another and share ideas.

Church and Nonprofit Over the Long Haul

Starting a church-based nonprofit is a "long haul" kind of action. It is like adding a family member that will hopefully grow *and* retain strong ties to the family. Over the years, the community may change around both the church and the nonprofit, meaning that leadership will need to be open to a new focus and strategies. What your nonprofit is doing today may not be relevant in a few years when the economy and demographics of your community change. It is also true that church-nonprofit relationships often evolve over the years. As your nonprofit grows, it may be less dependent on the church for volunteers and funding. And as the nonprofit develops community partnerships, some programs may be developed with less involvement from the church. So be prepared to have an ongoing conversation about how the nonprofit uses its resources and works together with the church.

What You'll Need

- A team of staff and lay leaders to serve as the steering committee that will bring the nonprofit into being
- The administrative/management skills required to run a separate organization (not present in all churches!)
- Legal help to complete the state and federal nonprofit paperwork
- Willing people to serve as your first board of directors

- At least one person on the church staff who can devote time to forming and overseeing the nonprofit, even if just a few hours a week
- Strong communication between the church and nonprofit at the outset and ongoing

PART THREE

Moving Forward on Your Ministry Dream

Choosing a Model for Ministry

As you develop your plan for new community ministry, you will need to choose a model along the way or two or more models to fit together into a hybrid approach. Choosing a model involves taking a hard look at the capacity of your congregation (both strengths and weaknesses) and determining the type of church you are—partner, or advocate entrepreneur, congregation. Also, you will need to develop a process for deciding on a model and a focus for your new ministry.

What Type of Church Are You?

Thinking about the "ministry DNA" of your church can help you choose a model. How is it that you typically "do ministry"? Are you more likely to partner or start your own ministries from scratch? Or maybe your congregation is all about advocating—digging deep into the structural issues that cause poverty and racism, for example. I have identified three "types" of churches below and the community ministry models they are most likely to have the skills, interest, and passion to implement. It is possible that your congregation has elements of all three present in your ministries; however, as you read the descriptions below, one will probably jump out at you as being more descriptive of your church than the other two.

The Partnering Church

Orientation toward Model 1: "Donate Goods or Money"; Model 2: "Mobilize Volunteers"; and Model 3: "Partner with Other Organizations"

Moses decided to partner when the job of judging the people's disputes became too large for just one man. Moses sat from the early morning hours until evening every day serving as judge. His father-in-law, Jethro, said to him, "What you are doing is not good. You will surely wear yourself out, both you and these people with you. For the task is too heavy for you; you cannot do it alone" (Exodus 18:17-18). He instructed Moses to "look for able men among all the people. . . . It will be easier for you, and they will bear the burden with you. . . . Then you will be able to endure" (verses 21-23). Moses took this opportunity for partnership, collaborating by appointing other leaders over "thousands, hundreds, fifties, and tens" of the people, requiring them to bring only the important cases to him (verses 25-26).

Maybe, like Moses, your church realizes that your vision for ministry is bigger than your congregation alone can handle. As a partnering church, you are always looking for new ways to work with others. Many ministry programs at your church are done in collaboration with outside organizations or with other ministry departments within your church. People in your church are connectors—they have extensive networks of contacts that they would like to connect your congregation to. Many of your congregation members may work in sales or communications or have jobs in public schools, government, or the nonprofit sector that require them to be good at finding and connecting resources. If you are a staff member at a church and your members are always trying to get you to attend lunch meetings of their club, association, or nonprofit group, then your church might be a partnering church.

Partnering churches are exceptional at doing the following:

- Identifying how partnerships can benefit ministry. Often, people in your church see the missing piece of your ministry that a partner could provide.
- Looking at ministry as a way to draw people and organizations together. (You might find yourselves saying "we" and "ours" rather than "me" and "my.")

- Maximizing both human and financial resources. People in your church believe strongly in not duplicating efforts, and they see the importance of pooling resources with other groups.
- Sharing. Church members are excited about sharing things like buildings, volunteers, equipment, staff, relationships, and funding.
- Developing and drawing upon networks of potential partners. Church members are always on the lookout for partners and enjoy attending events and participating in networks where potential partners could be found.
- Negotiating with partners to define how your church and the partner fit together. Working out the details of a partnership takes patience, and your church members are up to the task. You'll need to work out who is responsible for delivering programs, providing space and funding, recruiting and training volunteers, and promoting the program, among other details.

REDEEMER LUTHERAN CHURCH AND REDEEMER CENTER FOR LIFE

Redeemer Lutheran Church and the nonprofit it founded, Redeemer Center for Life, embody the elements of the partnering church. Both organizations make a significant impact in the Harrison neighborhood of North Minneapolis through the relationships they have formed with a variety of partners.

Marilu Thomas, former executive director of RCFL, says that the most important factor in selecting partners is to find people and groups who share your values. "We value relationships, and so [we] need to partner with other groups that value relationships. . . . Once we know that we share values, we look for groups that have capacity and expertise that we don't have." RCFL also puts a particular value on education as a way to stop the cycle of generational poverty, so partnering with educational institutions comes naturally.

Currently they have partnerships with Lutheran colleges in the area as well as the University of Minnesota, which helped RCFL set up the Venture North Bike Shop, provided entrepreneurial training for youth, and sent VISTA volunteers to help with summer camps. RCFL health programs are done in partnership with the major health organizations in the Twin Cities as well as community clinics. Other partners have included Lutheran Social Services (providing financial literacy training in the neighborhood), the local neighborhood association (organizes neighbors on public policy issues), and a host of partner churches that send more than three hundred volunteers a year to help at the church and nonprofit.

Pastor Kelly Chatman, pastor of Redeemer Lutheran Church, said that the key to strong partnerships is reciprocity, relationship, and transformation. Redeemer's partnerships with suburban churches, for example, are all about a two-way exchange. "There's a danger that the partner with the resources is seen as the only one who is giving—but we need equity for a strong partnership—both partners need to give," he said. In developing relationships with partner churches, Redeemer invites suburban church members to worship at Redeemer on Sunday mornings. "I think worshipping with us helped bring them out of the 'we-they' mentality. We are inviting our suburban partners into the transforming reality of participating with another community." Suburban church members are invited to the annual block party and other special events and work side by side with volunteers from the neighborhood in the after-school program. Some partner churches have played major roles in rehabbing housing and program space. "We create opportunities so that people can see the change in their own lives and the difference that ministry makes in their lives and in the lives of the people they are working with," Chatman said.

The Advocate Church

Orientation toward Model 4: "Advocate around Public Policy" and Model 5: "Engage in Community Organizing"

Huldah, one of the few female prophets mentioned in the Bible, advised King Josiah about implementing the newly discovered Book of the Law for the sake of reforming the kingdom of Judah. It could be a risky thing for a prophet to speak honestly to the king, but the great prophets, those who were true to their calling, spoke out for the sake of God's people. Huldah had the courage to advocate for reform despite the implicit criticism that she communicated about the king's reign. Her honest critique and advocacy empowered Josiah to turn the kingdom away from worshipping many gods (a long-held practice) and toward worshipping the one true God (see 2 Kings 22; 2 Chronicles 34).

Your congregation may be like Huldah, in that you are advocates for true reform. Your congregation is passionate about influencing the structures and policies that are root causes of the challenges faced by your community. People outside your congregation might say you are a "social justice" church. When you have conversations at your church about what you could do to serve the community, people are much less likely to express interest in "hands-on" service and more likely to ask questions about how people and policies could be influenced to achieve a more permanent change.

Church members are well-informed about community issues and are especially interested in situations where people are being marginalized or discriminated against. You might have people in your church who work directly on justice issues—people such as lawyers, parole officers, or social workers who work at the juvenile detention center, who see with their own eyes the results of unjust policies and systems. If you look back at the history of your congregation, it is likely you will see significant engagement in justice issues of the day. Maybe your church was instrumental in civil rights activities in your community, providing people, financial resources, space for meetings, or a voice through the pulpit for the movement.

Advocate congregations are especially good at the following:

- Seeing deeper than the problem at hand—understanding how structures, policies, and bureaucracies create injustices
- Being passionate about the disenfranchised and working to empower them
- Navigating high-conflict situations where many of the players disagree with each other
- Understanding how political systems and other bureaucracies operate and how they can be influenced
- Working together with a diversity of people for a cause— crossing racial, socioeconomic, religious, and political boundaries to build relationships and coalitions
- Communicating about social justice issues in an inspiring way that draws other people in

HOLY TRINITY LUTHERAN CHURCH: DECADES OF ADVOCACY
Holy Trinity Lutheran Church in South Minneapolis has had advocacy as a part of its church life for decades. When the church

worked with a developer to construct new Section 8 (low income) housing on land owned by the church, congregation members saw the actual building of housing as just one part of their overall ministry approach. Church members also participated in a campaign to influence the legislature to approve more funding for affordable housing throughout the state. Another time church members were active (along with many other neighbors and organizations) in getting a notorious "sauna" shut down. It was located just two blocks from the church and was the reported site of many illegal activities, including prostitution. Also, the church successfully advocated for the location of a "halfway house" in the neighborhood, where people just coming out of prison could live, when many people in the neighborhood were opposed to the idea. An active Peace with Justice committee in the church organizes Bread for the World letter-writing campaigns, Day on the Hill visits with legislators, and participation in ecumenical advocacy days. The committee also hosts educational events at the church, shows films like *Food, Inc.* and *Heist*, and sponsors a book club, inviting all church members to read the same book together.

"When longtime members talk about the history of our church, some of these advocacy victories are always mentioned," said Rev. Jay Carlson, pastor of the church.

Now the church has begun a new focus on community organizing as well, in addition to its longtime work on public policy. A part-time community organizer has been added to the church staff, and the congregation has begun to focus on actions it could take to curtail the activities of two payday lending institutions located near the church.

"We went to community organizing training together and began to see the differences between direct social service, advocacy, education, and direct-action organizing. We decided to take our existing commitments in a new direction, focusing on the organizing piece, without giving up what we were already doing," said Carlson. For Holy Trinity, organizing has added a new focus on building relationships in the community, also a component of empowering those most affected by the issues involved. "With public policy advocacy, you are lending your voice for those who have none; in organizing you are allowing those affected to use their voice," Carlson explained.

Organizing work started through one-on-one conversations between members of the church and neighborhood residents. Members also talked with potential partners in organizing work, including several large social service providers, an advocacy coalition, a local public school, and local businesses. Those interviewed said they saw food, education, and payday lending as key issues for the neighborhood.

The church decided to focus on payday lending and began by conducting extensive research into laws and regulations governing lending institutions. "Someone in the church read every book on the topic!" said Meghan Olsen-Biebighauser, community organizer at Holy Trinity. Church members met with legislators and sent letters to them urging reform. They are also beginning to talk about how to help create alternative lending opportunities for the community, recognizing that many families do have a need for emergency loans from time to time. Most recently, Holy Trinity was awarded a $50,000 grant through a partner church to fund the start-up of an alternative lending program. The new focus on lending practices and options is just one initiative in the church's long history of advocacy.

The Entrepreneurial Church

Orientation toward Model 6: "Develop a Ministry Program" and Model 7: "Create a Church-Based Nonprofit"

Paul was the classic ministry entrepreneur, seeking new ground for the church, innovating ministries, and engaging new people wherever he went on his missionary journeys in Asia, Europe, and the Middle East. He had a big vision for the church, challenging disciples to be faithful and grow their numbers. He called believers to engage with the world and build bridges with people of many nations and cultures.

Maybe, like Paul, your church is imbued with a vision for new ministry. Your congregation just can't stop creating new things. People in the church are full of ideas; many of them may be entrepreneurs in business or creative types (writers, media professionals, artists). New ministry burgeons constantly. Your pastor or other leaders may have a far-off, seemingly unattainable vision of a much larger organization with many sites, or of a replication model that would involve starting more ministries like yours in other locations. Church planting may be in the DNA of your church—even if it is far back in the congregation's history.

Entrepreneurial churches are exceptional at doing these kinds of things:

- Developing vision for new ministry
- Seeing what is possible, even if it looks really different than what is present today at your church. You are good at drawing a picture of the programs and organizations that could spring forth from your church.
- Thinking differently, developing new patterns or models of ministry
- Thinking strategically about how and when to implement new ministry
- Developing detailed plans for implementing the vision
- Building capacity to implement the plan, including drawing in the right people
- Communicating about the vision so that new resources can be raised

SHILOH TEMPLE: DEVELOPING PEOPLE TO BE MINISTRY ENTREPRENEURS

Shiloh Temple International Ministries is an Apostolic Faith congregation located in North Minneapolis. Led by Bishop Richard Howell and Pastor Bettye Howell, the congregation has created myriad ministries to benefit the community and has planted seven new church congregations in the Twin Cities area. The congregation is known for its entrepreneurial nature and has pioneered many new ministries in a community that faces a variety of complex issues.

The church started a highly successful day care center in its building that serves the families of North Minneapolis. It also hosts a food shelf and clothing closet on-site and a reentry program for people coming out of prison that provides a support group and helps finding housing and employment. Community service liaisons employed by the church connect people to resources they need (like housing, employment, and rent assistance). The liaisons played an important role in connecting people to resources after a tornado struck North Minneapolis in the spring of 2011 and many families in the area were left homeless and without resources. The church has also started a variety of other community initiatives.

Bishop Howell's philosophy is that the "local church must be the hub of every community." Before launching new ministry programs, church staff and lay leaders spend a great deal of time learning about community issues. The church connects with church members who live and work in the community to monitor the pulse of the neighborhood. A close connection to neighborhood organizations and residents who live near the church has also been important. Using these techniques, the church identified a "youth gap" in education, mental health, and social behaviors—areas in which the church may develop new ministry.

A focus on the development of people has been key to the church's entrepreneurial focus. A hallmark of Shiloh's ministry is helping people to understand their gifts and abilities and equipping them to work in ministry that fits with how God made them. "Everyone has a genius in them," says Howell. "God placed it there to be developed." Church members participate in Bible studies and small groups designed to help them grow spiritually, identify God's call on their lives, and learn about leadership.

Bishop Howell says that one key to bringing new visions into reality is to find the "vision pushers" in the congregation. "Visionaries are not vision pushers," he said. "Vision pushers can see what the vision is and know what needs to be done to implement it." Teams are formed around each ministry idea, tasked with doing research on the community and the program model, developing a plan, and organizing resources.

In the case of the day care center, a team comprised of church staff, teachers from the congregation, and mothers from the community worked for more than a year to research the idea and develop a plan. The result is a successful center that is led by people who were developed as leaders in this entrepreneurial church.

Take a Hard Look at Your Capacity

Another strategy in choosing a model is to take a hard look at the capacity of your congregation. This is the pragmatic aspect of developing new ministry, when you "walk on the ground" and look honestly at what your congregation could actually implement. Can you recruit volunteers and raise money? Is planning a particular strength of your congregation? How do you do on completing detailed administrative tasks? Answers to these kinds of questions ought to influence the model you choose.

These conversations about capacity can be difficult if your church isn't used to talking about what *hasn't* worked over the years, something that is as important as (if not more important than) understanding what your congregation is good at. Sometimes the process of really talking to each other about capacity issues is an outcome in itself—and more honest conversations become possible in the future. I find in my work that people are often relieved to have these conversations. They have been wondering for a long time (maybe years) about how ministry could be strengthened or why certain efforts seem to fail, but they may have been too reticent to ask. So if you are nervous about bringing this up, just know that it might be easier to have the conversation than you think.

I have noted in each model chapter what is required to implement that particular model. Below are some broader questions to ask as you assess, realistically, what can be implemented in your church.

The big picture: What is your congregation especially good at? Take a step back and look at the most successful ministries in your church. Why do they work? They might succeed because of some of the following characteristics of your congregation:

- "Big idea" people with vision who can champion the cause
- An exceptionally gifted administrative staff who run with the plans that are developed and implement details
- Financially generous members who are willing to dig deep when new opportunities for ministry arise
- A core group of dedicated volunteers who have been successful at recruiting others to get involved
- A pastor who can generate interest in new ministry through compelling biblical preaching and teaching

Where do you lack skills and expertise? Now take a hard look at ministries that seem to struggle and never get off the ground.

Every church has them. Ask some hard questions about why. Here are some examples of why ministries fail:

- Your church tends to start new ministries whether or not the "content" expertise is present in the congregation—for example, starting an after-school program without anyone present who has a youth development or education background.
- Your church tends to create ministries from scratch when partnering with another organization would make more sense.
- You struggle with the administrative side of ministry—coordinating schedules, completing paperwork, communicating with volunteers, forming committees and boards and getting them together for meetings.
- Your church has great vision but little ability to plan.
- Recruiting volunteers is difficult—everyone says they are too busy to get involved or no one follows up with the people who do sign up to volunteer.
- One or more church staff members resist the development of new ministry.

As you look at where you lack capacity, consider whether these are areas where you could improve with new strategies or training or through partnerships. Deciding that you just aren't gifted in an area will inform the model you choose.

How much staff time can be devoted to new community ministry? Most new community ministry efforts require at least some involvement of church staff at the outset. Sometimes staff spend a great deal of time working on new ministry—serving as primary leaders as new programs and partnerships are developed and communicated to the congregation. But even in efforts led by lay leaders, it can be important for staff to be present (at least initially) to make sure that new ministry is developed in alignment with the broader vision of the church.

So if your current staff is completely taxed, unable to add one more thing to their schedules, that will influence what you are able to develop and launch.

Are people in your church likely to volunteer? Some of the models in this book are more "volunteer intensive" than others, so assessing how many volunteers you can likely recruit from your congregation is a part of assessing capacity. Do you have a committed group of volunteers right now? If so, are they usually able to recruit others to help as needed? What is the typical response to your efforts to recruit volunteers? Choose a less volunteer intensive approach if you have trouble recruiting volunteers.

Keep in mind that even if few church members have been willing to engage as volunteers, you may be able to strengthen your volunteer program so that more members respond (see Model 2: "Mobilize Volunteers").

How much money can you raise for new community ministry, both inside and outside of your church? Models 6 and 7 tend to have greater up-front financial costs associated with them than the other models, as you are developing programming on-site that is being run by your church. Costs might include additional staff positions, equipment and supplies for programming, filing fees for incorporation, increased insurance costs, and expenses related to technology and communications (business cards, flyers, web design, etc.). So ask yourself whether people in your church have the capacity to give more. How do they typically respond to special appeals? Could more be done to encourage greater giving?

Also think about how you might attract funding from outside your congregation—foundation and corporate grants, government support, or funding from church partners or individuals outside your church (see "Securing Funds for Your Ministry" in Part Three). People in your church with fund-raising expertise (as a paid professional or volunteer) could help you assess your capacity here, or you might be able to find a fund-raising professional in your community who would be willing to listen to your ministry idea and give you an honest opinion. Of course, you could also hire a fund-raising consultant to assess your fund-raising capacity and develop a fund-raising plan.

Tips on Process and Communication

Choosing a model for ministry has tremendous implications—for your congregation and for the new ministry programs you are deciding to implement. Whatever you choose, make sure you involve a group of people in making the choice and make a commitment to communicate well to your congregation along the way. Here are a few tips on process and communication.

Involve a Group of People in Developing Recommendations

New ministries often begin with the vision and enthusiasm of just a couple of individuals, but to launch and sustain a ministry, you will need more participants than that. Consider forming a group of eight to ten people who will carefully take a look at the ministry idea and develop recommendations to be considered by your elected church leaders, or perhaps by the whole congregation (if you use a congregational model).

Group process takes longer (and can make visionary types feel impatient!), but the end product is often better. With a larger group, you could bring your visionaries together with planners, technicians, organizers, and content experts (in education, health, or housing, for example), and examine the idea from a wide variety of angles.

Keep Leaders in the Loop

Make sure the key leaders in your congregation are kept informed of your progress throughout the process of choosing a model. Key leaders would obviously include key staff members—your senior pastor (of course) and staff members who are involved in ministry that might be related to the new ministry you are developing. Members of the church governing board or council should be kept in the loop too, as well as "informal" leaders with a lot of influence—people who may not have an official title or role but whom the people in the church listen to, perhaps because of their "elder" status, expertise, or sacrifices they have made for the congregation in the past (for example, chairing the board through a particularly rocky time).

Communicate with the Entire Congregation

Part of your process should be to develop a communication strategy for how the congregation will find out about the development and launch of the new ministry. It is better to communicate more rather than less. Even new ideas that seem to be "controversy-free" can cause a rift if inaccurate information is floating around. Even if something is just being discussed or is in the very early stages of development, you can communicate that to the congregation: "We want you to know that a group has been appointed to look at the formation of a separate nonprofit organization connected to our congregation. We are now looking at models being used by other churches and will be reporting our findings at the annual meeting in March." That kind of communication can help prevent people from leaping to the conclusion that the ministry is ready to launch and no one bothered to tell them about it.

Communicate more about the models that require the church to take more risks and/or expend more resources. Models 6 and 7 in this book (Develop a Ministry Program and Create a Church-Based Nonprofit) often take more resources to implement than the other models and typically require a church to take more risks. With programming that you run yourselves, operating at your location, there are liability risks, financial risks, and risks to the church's reputation if things don't go well. These models also tend to take more resources to implement than the other models—space, staff time, use of equipment and supplies, and also volunteers. The process for giving the green light to these models ought to take longer, and informing your congregation at various points in the process will help head off misunderstandings and gradually build support for the launching of a new ministry (or a new nonprofit). When considering starting your own program on-site, for example, you might inform the congregation after these steps are completed:

- We learned the following things about our community.
- We have an idea for a new ministry program that could be offered at our church.
- We found a partner that is willing to work with us on implementing a new program at our church.
- Here is the plan for our new ministry.
- We would like the congregation to help us in the following ways with the new ministry.
- Here are ways that you can help us with the new ministry.

Hybrids Are Possible

If you have read this book chapter by chapter so far, you have probably recognized more than one community ministry model that your congregation is using or would like to use. This is normal! The models aren't intended to be exclusive of one another—a number of them fit together quite well. For example, Model 3 ("Partner with Other Organizations") often incorporates Model 1 ("Donate Goods or Money") and Model 2 ("Mobilize Volunteers"). Model 7 ("Create a Church-Based Nonprofit") usually means that your church has or will implement Model 6 ("Develop a Ministry Program") so that there are some programs to put into the nonprofit or that will be started under the nonprofit.

It is also true that churches often start with one model and add others as they learn more about the community and the capacity and passions of their congregation. Here are two examples:

Donating goods leads to developing your own program. Your congregation starts its community ministry efforts by collecting food to donate to the food shelf in a nearby town. As you develop a relationship with the staff of the food shelf, you hear from them that they are at capacity and serve many people from your town. Many of these folks have transportation issues that make it difficult for them to get food from a pantry that is far away from where they live. Because of what you learned by implementing Model 1, your church decides to open its own food shelf (Model 6) to serve the people from your community.

Partnership leads to public policy advocacy. Your church partners with a local public school that doesn't have enough resources. Volunteers from your church go in every week to tutor students in reading and math. You collect school supplies and winter coats and help out with the school carnival, the spaghetti dinner, and the book fair. People from your church are in the school every week, observing the lack of resources, the struggles of students, and the difficulties teachers and administrators face in trying to do their jobs. When a new school referendum is placed on the ballot, some of your faithful school volunteers encourage your congregation to take a stand on the issue. Your church works with the Good Schools Network (a local advocacy group) to educate your congregation.

No One Right Answer

There are no "one size fits all" answers for congregations seeking to start new community ministry. That is why it is important to devote some time at the outset to thinking through and praying through the model that is the best fit for your congregation, even if the process of thinking, weighing, and deciding makes some people impatient. The greatest ministry ideas might press on you to push the start button immediately. But the time you spend considering the models will be worth it and will lead to ministry that is more sustainable for your congregation.

Measuring Success in Your Ministry

What does success in community ministry look like? And how do you know if you've gotten there? These are important questions to discuss as you choose your model and develop your ministry plan.

In community ministry, measuring success ought to be far different than the "more, bigger, faster" measures that are used so often in our culture to assess progress. I would argue that these measures should not be our focus in the church, where Christ often calls his followers to slow, steady, consistent work, perhaps with a small group of people, at least to start. In my experience, the best community ministry programs are often small (or at least start that way) and take awhile to develop.

The Importance of Outcomes

To accurately measure the success of your ministry work, you will need to start thinking about outcomes—if you haven't already. Outcomes are the ultimate impact that your work has on the people involved. Outcomes answer the question "What changes in the world because of our work?" Outcomes vary from ministry to ministry.

For example, if you decide to partner with a local public school, you might be trying to achieve outcomes for individual students and parents, the entire school or community, and your church members. Following are some typical outcomes:

- Tutors from our church helped children improve their reading and math skills.
- Volunteers from our church provided a consistent and positive adult presence for the students at the school by serving as "lunch buddies."
- Our work at special events increased the number of parents attending parent-teacher conferences. As a result, parents helped their children complete homework on a more consistent basis.
- Students had a safe place to be after school because our church started and staffed a daily after-school program.
- Church members who volunteered gained a new understanding of how Christian faith is tied to working toward justice in the community. This spurred church members to engage in other community transformation projects.
- Several other churches sent in volunteer tutors to the school because our work drew community-wide attention to the school's needs.

Depending on which outcomes you choose from the list above, you might focus your efforts on recruiting and training tutors, raising money, or organizing special events. Too often churches lurch forward into new community ministry programs without discussing what success looks like. Without a conversation about outcomes, it is easy to go through the motions, just generating more and more programming, without really thinking about the intended benefit for community members—and church members as well. The result is often no results, because ministry was not designed with the end outcome in mind.

Without outcomes, the people in your church involved in community ministry may begin to work at cross-purposes to each other, each having a different idea of what your effort is trying to achieve. It could become more and more difficult to pull people together around the vision. Without outcomes, you will have no way to measure progress, so it may feel as though nothing is ever accomplished. This can be frustrating to both staff and volunteers—*We are putting in all of this work, and for what?* Outcomes may seem like a great deal of structure imposed on your creative ministry idea at first—maybe confining like "jail." But I have found that focusing on the end result actually brings freedom. You can be more focused on the work and stop wondering, *What are we aiming for?*

What Changes in the World Because of Your Work?

Outcomes are not just a listing of events or activities—"We facilitated six block club meetings," "We offered three tutoring sessions," or "We helped out at the food shelf five times this month." And they're not just a numerical counting either—"We mobilized a hundred volunteers to serve at the Union Gospel Mission," "A hundred kids went to camp," or "Three hundred adults and children received flu shots." Keeping track of the activities you offer and the number of people served is important, but doing that doesn't really measure impact.

What I am talking about is transformation of people. If you were tutoring youth, for example, your outcome wouldn't just be "Twenty youth participate in our tutoring program." Instead, you should identify the specific academic benefit you want the youth to achieve. You might consider the following kinds of outcomes:

- Short-term: Reading skills improve.
- Short-term: Youth complete their homework.
- Mid-term: Youth express more interest in school and have greater participation in the classroom.
- Long-term: Youth graduate from high school.
- Long-term: Youth go on to college.

Outcomes Influence Program Design

Identifying your outcomes ought to influence your program design. So in a program designed to help youth improve their reading skills, you would expect to find youth spending a lot of time reading or working through a reading skills curriculum on the computer or receiving one-on-one tutoring focused on reading. Making sure there is a match between your intended outcomes and your program design is one of the most important aspects of putting together a community ministry plan.

I once worked with a ministry to the homeless that had an expressed mission of helping people move from homelessness to stability. Their vision was that program participants would eventually become employed and have stable housing. However, when we looked at the content of this group's programming, we saw that 75 percent of it was focused on helping people meet basic needs for food and clothing. Only 25 percent of the program was focused on helping people develop skills and get connected to resources so they could move forward toward housing and employment. Identifying their outcomes clearly helped this group flip the emphasis in their programs so that there was alignment between desired outcomes and program design.

Measuring Outcomes in Your Community

So what would real results look like in the community where you are ministering? There aren't just a few kinds of community outcomes that can be achieved through community ministry; there are many. So don't just think that all ministries should focus on "people getting jobs" or "kids graduating from high school." Sometimes I work with congregations that aim for something they think they "ought to" focus on. Instead, use the "Meeting the Neighbors" process (see pages 11–27) to help you surface the kinds of impacts and outcomes your community really needs. To get you started thinking about how you might set and measure outcomes, I have developed a list of the kinds of impact your ministry might have in the community.

Economic Outcomes

One set of outcomes focuses on the economic well-being of the people in your community—how your ministry might impact their ability to earn and save money so they can meet basic needs and move forward toward self-sufficiency and success.

The vision. People in your community are in a better position to succeed economically because of your ministry. They can support their families and are not only able to meet basic needs but are able to save assets in order to secure long-term financial success (buying a house or investing in retirement funds, for example) and to help the next generation (saving for college, for example).

The ministries. Ministries to achieve economic outcomes might include developing new businesses that create new jobs, constructing affordable housing, developing a transitional housing program, providing job training in specific fields like construction or the culinary arts, and teaching classes on résumé writing and job search.

To make an economic impact in your community, your ministry might work toward the following outcomes:

- People gain access to employment through the creation of new jobs in the community (small business development and attraction of large-scale employers to the community).
- Residents secure employment because they receive job training and coaching on the job search process.
- Residents purchase homes because they are able to secure low-interest loans.
- Families better manage the resources they have and invest for the future because of what they learn through financial management training.

Educational Outcomes

Many churches and nonprofits work on educational outcomes focused on helping people complete schooling and get other kinds of training. Educational outcomes can be tied to economic outcomes but are also a set of results in and of themselves.

The vision. All residents complete K–12 educational requirements and go on to get the training and education they need to secure living wage employment.

The ministries. Ministries to achieve educational outcomes could include offering English as a second language (ESL) and graduate equivalency diploma (GED) classes at your church, providing volunteer reading and math tutors at the local public school, offering a college prep course that includes college tours, and providing help in completing college applications and preparing for college-readiness tests.

Following are some outcomes for your church to work on:

- Immigrants improve their English skills through ESL classes.
- Elementary school children meet or exceed standards in their math and reading skills through a tutoring program staffed by volunteers from your church.
- High school students complete requirements and graduate from high school on time.

- High school students get ready for the college search and application process through test preparation, college tours, and applying for financial aid.
- Adults without high school diplomas get their GED certificates through a program at your church.

Relationship/Social Outcomes

These are a set of outcomes that many congregations miss. People need relationships to succeed in life. Your network of relationships (also called your "social capital") can help you get connected to things you need—housing, jobs, educational opportunities, transportation, and people who can teach you what you need to know. People who live in poverty often lack these types of relationships and need to build them to move on to a better life.

The vision. People have opportunities to connect with a diversity of people from their community and possess skills and interest in developing new relationships.

The ministries. Ministries that achieve relationship and social outcomes could include a mentoring program that pairs youth with adults, a network of block clubs that bring neighbors together on a regular basis, and affinity groups for like-minded people in the community—a runners group, gardeners club, or artists salon. They could also include convening residents to work together on community issues like advocating to keep the local public park open.

Outcomes of your ministry could include these:

- Adults and youth form mentoring relationships. The adults share their knowledge and experience of educational and career success and model positive personal relationships.
- People are provided with opportunities to get connected to others who have resources they need—jobs, housing, information, and so on—both inside and outside the community.
- People form teams or groups, including block clubs or neighborhood associations, to work on a community issue together.
- Residents learn how to share skills and expertise with one another—such as home repair, cooking, car repair, or babysitting.

- Residents form social bonds with one another, as evidenced by the fact that they create regular opportunities to get together.

Health Outcomes

Good physical and mental health can enable you to move forward on all of the other outcomes described so far in this chapter; poor health can stand in the way.

The vision. People experience physical and emotional well-being, enabling them to work toward their goals in life.

The ministries. To achieve health outcomes, your church might offer regular exercise classes to the community, host a community garden and healthy cooking classes, partner with your local hospital to offer a clinic on-site, or offer health checks for diabetes and high blood pressure at community events.

Outcomes of your ministry could include the following:

- Lower disease rates in the community. Fewer people in your community develop diabetes or have high blood pressure.
- Increase in healthy eating. More people from your community incorporate vegetables into their diets on a regular basis.
- More people from the community incorporate exercise into their daily lives.
- Development of greater "social capital" focused on health. People in your community develop "healthy living clubs"—small groups that get together regularly to exercise.
- Greater access to health care. More people in your community have access to health insurance and the medical care they need.

Institutional Outcomes

Building institutions in your community is also important. If schools, nonprofits, churches, and other organizations are strengthened as organizations, they are better able to help individuals and families achieve outcomes over the long-term.

The vision. Institutions in your community are strong and well-resourced, and they work to benefit the broader community.

The ministries. This may be a set of outcomes for your church if you are using a partnership approach and are mobilizing some of your volunteers to work on organizational issues with your partners (like fund-raising, planning, etc.). Your work with other organizations could result in a permanent change in your partners' capacity to do their work.

Institutional outcomes might include these:

- Creation of a strategic plan that helps the organization move forward
- A stronger board through adding new members (some from your church) and increasing board effectiveness through training
- Increased fund-raising capacity that secures new grant funding and new support from individual donors
- Development of new human resource policies and practices, enabling the organization to secure qualified staff

The lists above are not intended to be exhaustive. There are many other types of programs and many other kinds of outcomes to go with them. These lists are intended to get you started thinking about outcomes for your proposed programming.

Ways to Measure Success

In addition to developing outcomes, you will need tools to help you measure whether or not you have met the outcomes. You will want to avoid creating an "evaluation bureaucracy"—a huge pile of forms for your volunteers and staff to fill out. Don't add administrative burden where you don't need to. If you can, do develop evaluation tools that fit right into the flow of your programming (or that of your partner).

In one of my church jobs, we sent girls on a bike trip every summer—250 miles in a week! We were just starting to develop evaluation tools, so I excitedly put together a written survey for every girl to complete at the end of the trip. When the group returned, I asked for the forms, but one of the counselors told me, "They got stuck to the bottom of the van with Kool-Aid and marshmallows!" This was an example of the wrong tool for the activity we were trying to evaluate. The next year, we decided to send pretty little journals with each girl and asked each one to complete a journal entry at the end of the day, describing what she had learned and how she had grown. The counselors looked through the journals at the end and pulled out key ideas. This was a much better tool to use under the circumstances—and the girls enjoyed their little books!

Here is another example of how you might build evaluation activities right into your program design. Let's say your youth development program has a focus on community service. Your measure of success may be that the youth successfully plan and execute a community service project—cleaning up a local park and installing playground equipment that the youth raised funds to purchase. You simply observe whether they are able to pull it off. Then you might ask the youth to reflect on what they learned through the process (perhaps through a group discussion or some journaling) and capture outcome data that way as well. You might also ask community residents about the impact on the neighborhood of a cleaner park with new equipment.

Tools to Measure Outcomes

A variety of tools can be used to measure outcomes. People often jump right to creating a written survey for participants to fill out. This may not be the best approach, in large part because most people don't like to complete paperwork. A number of other options described on these next pages may result in better data and may be more fun for your participants to complete. Some tools you will need to use both *before* embarking on a ministry project as well as *after* a predetermined period of time. Those tools measure change over time. Others you may use periodically to gather feedback and constructive critique of your ministry efforts.

Another thing to keep in mind: your funders may have expectations about how you will collect data about your results. This may be true of government agencies that provide funding as well as corporate, private, or community foundations. So check your grant agreements and contracts to see what your funders expect. Some grants may require you to use a particular assessment tool to measure such things as addiction recovery, reading skills, or level of self-esteem. Or you may be asked to collect certain kinds of statistics for your program—such as the ethnicity of participants or their income and education level.

Surveys of Knowledge

Using written assessments may be a good tool for you if you are focusing on educational goals and participants are expected to expand their knowledge. You could create your own simple surveys to assess knowledge—find out what participants learned about bike safety or interviewing for a new job, for example. You could also use tests developed by someone else—professionals in the program field in which you are working. Reading assessments (assessing grade level before and after the program) are a good example of this, as are evaluation tools to assess indicators of physical or mental health. Also, if you are partnering with another organization in programming, they may have assessment tools that they use.

Successful completion of a project. One church I worked for sponsored a canoe trip for middle school boys every summer. The boys developed a budget for the project, mapped out a route, purchased their supplies, and then went on the trip (doing all of this with the support of adult volunteers). I like to say that the outcome of that project was "They went into the woods, *and* they came out of the woods!" So simply observing if the project is completed is a measurement—housing was constructed; the community garden was planted and the vegetables were harvested; the youth completed the science experiments.

Focus groups. Focus groups are a way for you to talk directly to participants (and perhaps parents, volunteers, staff, and other important people) about the impact the program has had on their lives. Groups of seven to twelve people work best, and allow no more than ninety minutes for discussion. Depending on who you are meeting with (young children, for example), you may have much less time than that! Last year I facilitated a focus group with second graders. I had to bribe them with candy and only got in about twenty minutes of conversation, but they were able to tell us how the program had had an impact on them. (Hopefully you won't have to bribe your adult participants with candy!)

Consider using a facilitator for your groups, someone who will lead the sessions and ensure that everyone has a chance to contribute. It is helpful to choose facilitators who are not involved in the program so that group participants will give honest answers. You may even want to consider hiring an outside person to conduct the groups—a neutral third party who has no stake in the answers people give. Avoid a situation where focus group participants feel nervous about being honest because they know the facilitator and don't want to hurt his or her feelings, or worse, are concerned that the facilitator might retaliate in some way if negative comments are made (such as not allowing participants to continue in the program).

One-on-one interviews. Sitting down with program participants one-on-one often yields the most detailed and honest information compared to other tools. Focus your questions on the impact the program has had on the person's life: "Tell me two or three things you learned through this program." "What did you learn here that you used at home, school, or someplace else?" "What have you learned here that has helped you to be more successful in school?" Again, it is helpful to have someone who is not the program leader conduct the interviews—more honest dialogue results when people don't feel pressure to be positive.

Observation. Another way to measure outcomes is to ask staff and volunteers to observe change in program participants over time. Staff and volunteers could be asked to write down a brief synopsis of each session, for example, commenting on what they think participants learned and also how they have changed over a period of time. In a job search program, for example, staff may be able to note how one participant has improved his or her interviewing skills over the course of the program.

It Takes a Long Time to Get There

Many church leaders have told me they get impatient waiting for success in community ministry. Your long-term outcome of community transformation, high school graduation, or employment for community residents may take awhile to achieve. When church and community members expect success quickly, part of your job will be to help them adjust expectations to see that it is not just the long-term successes that count. There will be many small successes along the way.

When working with the homeless, for example, small successes along the way often add up to the big success down the road of employment and stable housing. I have worked with several large ministries to the homeless here in the Twin Cities, and their benchmarks for participants include small successes such as these:

- Research a list of organizations that could help you get your GED.
- Contact three organizations on the list to talk with them about how you might get your GED.
- Make appointments with three of the organizations.
- Show up to the appointments.
- Complete the paperwork you need to get accepted into the GED program.
- Show up to the first class, the next class, and the next class.
- Complete your homework for each session.

I like to think of measuring outcomes as driving down a road that has signposts on it. Participants are driving down the road, and sometimes their pace quickens; other times it slows; and sometimes they slide backward and have to "redo" parts of the road. This is particularly true of vulnerable people who may face challenges like addictions or mental health diagnoses. Their road to success may include many twists and turns, but that doesn't mean they won't make it all the way to the end.

Another example of a project that takes time is if your church decides to work on economic development in your community. It can take a long time, in part, because so many parties have to sign on to get the work done. So if your church is working on revitalizing a commercial corridor in a city neighborhood, for example, don't just consider the only success as a fully revitalized street with every storefront full and all of the buildings restored. Many small successes will occur along the way.

First and foremost would be the coming together of many different kinds of people from the community to work on the project. People often have to build relational bridges and develop new alliances to get this kind of work done. So the relationships formed are an outcome in themselves. Those relationships could lead to other kinds of work getting accomplished even after the project is completed—another outcome.

Small victories along the way may lead to a fully developed commercial corridor:

- The renovation of one key property on the street
- Commitments from one or two major funders to support the project
- Several new businesses leasing storefronts
- A major new retail tenant signing a lease

The reality of the fact that "it takes a long time" should be part of your planning process for community ministry. Help your church members see the success step-by-step even if the steps are small. If they are coached to take the long view from the start, church members will be less impatient and more willing to stay engaged, even in the face of setbacks.

Measuring Outcomes in Your Church

When you set outcomes for your community ministry program, you should also discuss outcomes of the ministry for your church members. Good community ministry ought to have strong, positive impacts on the community outside your church as well as on the people inside your church. Consider the following kinds of outcomes for church members as you put together your ministry plan.

Enhanced Cross-Cultural Skills

Community work can provide an opportunity for church members to learn about new cultures and develop new skills in working cross-culturally. In the book of Acts and Paul's letters, we get a clear picture of Christians embracing their multiethnic communities, building relationships cross-culturally, and doing the hard work of learning about each other. Working cross-culturally in community ministry, your church members can be equipped to live out their faith like those in the early church. Up close to another culture, building relationships with people who are very different from them, your church members may learn about the following things:

- The struggles immigrants face when coming to a new country
- How to introduce themselves to persons from other cultures
- Family structures and traditions, including the roles of men and women
- Holiday traditions and cultural events that are important in other cultures
- Food traditions. As you build relationships cross-culturally, you will no doubt be invited to events where food is served and may get to taste many new things.

New Eyes for the Community

Once they start getting to know the community, church members may actually see something different than they used to when they look out into it. Instead of seeing total despair, brokenness, basically *nothing*, they may begin to see capacity, ideas, and small successes happening every day. My husband said that he knew that he had new eyes for our community when he would bristle at news reports that focused only on murder and mayhem. Because he had built many relationships in our community, he knew there was much to tell about hardworking residents, engaged parents, and successful institutions. That news just didn't make it into the papers.

Relationship-Building Skills

Community ministry can better equip church members to form relationships—not only with community members but with other church members. Relational ministries, in particular, can help people become better listeners and communicators. Other relationship skills that may be developed include patience, encouragement, empathy, flexibility, courage, and candor, as well as being able to take risks and expose one's real self.

When church members work together on a community initiative, they also have opportunities to develop new and deeper relationships with each other. People who don't even know each other, and who have not had an interest in knowing each other, may come together around their passion for a particular community initiative. Ideas are shared that wouldn't have been, and people mentor and teach each other, beginning to run together toward the ministry goal.

A few times I have had to work on a community ministry effort with people I thought I didn't even like then found out they weren't so bad! They had gifts I hadn't noticed before but soon grew to appreciate; some of these people even became friends. Your church members may carry these new relationships and alliances into other work at the church, helping other ministry areas to become more productive.

Stronger Ministry Skills

Church members may end up with new hands-on skills in a ministry area, such as youth development or early childhood education. They may learn to be job coaches, ESL teachers, tutors, mentors, and volunteer construction workers. After they have been serving for a period of time, ask church members, "What have you learned about _____ (you fill in the blank: early childhood education, tutoring, affordable housing, etc.) that you didn't know before?" and "What can you do now that you couldn't do before?"

Stronger Leadership Ability

It is very possible that launching community ministry will grow leaders in your church. You will need to "give away" large pieces of developing and running the ministry to your lay leaders in order to achieve this outcome. If you see church members growing in the following areas, you will know that you are growing leaders:

- The courage to step in where there is a need
- The ability to look at the big picture, not just at areas of personal interest
- The ability to inspire people and draw them toward the vision
- Perception of barriers or boundaries and the willingness to breach them
- The courage to speak truth at the right times, even when it is hard and uncomfortable

- The ability to accept criticism—or disregard it (that is, develop a thick skin)
- A strong faith in God's leading and faithfulness

Spiritual Strengthening

Launching into community ministry in new ways can also be a real faith builder for your church members. Every new community ministry effort that I have been involved in has led me into new kinds of Scripture study, new ways of praying, and new ways of understanding how God works through me and the church. In these new endeavors, it is often hard to see what is down at the end of the road. We need to listen closely to God to see the next steps along the way.

Participation in Service in Other Areas of Life

Another outcome of community ministry: church members become more service-oriented in other areas of their lives outside of church. Working on community ministry ought to give church members new eyes for the community so they can notice needs and assets and consider how they could engage. So be sure to ask about where else people connect because you got them serving in the church. Done right, your community ministry volunteers ought to be signing up as Little League coaches, neighborhood watch captains, scout troop leaders, and board members of local nonprofits. This is a ripple effect of good community ministry.

Outcomes Will Set You Free

Establishing outcomes at the beginning of your ministry planning process will help you see where you are trying to go and aid you in designing an initiative that will help you get there. This is kind of like setting up the posts where the finish line will be so that you know which way to run. Put some thought into setting outcomes for your community—how will the community and the people in it change because of your work? But just as important are the outcomes for your church members. How will your efforts help them develop spiritually, learn new skills, and strengthen your congregation?

Securing Funds for Your Ministry

Some community ministry takes very little money to operate. You might be able to run your community program on the energy of volunteers and donated goods. But if your ministry grows to the point that you want to hire staff, rent space, or buy a lot of supplies and equipment, you're going to need to find some money.

Standing at the very beginning of the fund-raising process can be humbling. You will probably feel like you don't know what you are doing at first, but trust me, you can figure this out! It is generally true that the more you fund-raise, the better you get at it. And one of the great advantages of having to raise money is that it forces you to plan out and document your ministry ideas, and a well-planned ministry is usually more successful. So as you start this process, get ready to write down the details of all aspects of your ministry—its goals and outcomes, the when, where, why, how, and with whom aspects, and the compelling reasons for the ministry to exist at all.

Working toward a Broad Funding Base

Most people want to receive one big grant that will make all of their fund-raising worries go away. This would be ideal—right? You could get your big donation at the beginning of the year and then not worry about fund-raising again until next year. But the problem with one big grant is when the one big grant goes away.

Then your organization or program goes away. If you work toward a broad funding base, with different types of funders giving at many different levels, you can weather the storm when some funding disappears each year, which it inevitably will as people and institutions change their interests, move away, or die.

So if you were trying to raise $100,000 for your organization in the course of a year, the ideal scenario would be for you to have funding that is spread out among a few different sources. Consider the following example of fund-raising targets for securing $100,000 from a broad funding base:

Foundation and corporate grants—$50,000 in restricted funds (Note: Most grants these days go to support specific programs.)
- □ $20,000 from First Corp for the after-school tutoring program
- □ $10,000 from Universal Health for the annual health fair
- □ $10,000 from Bank of the Region for summer camp scholarships
- □ $5,000 from the City Community Foundation to help cover the cost of a new case manager who will work with families
- □ Two $2,500 gifts from local bank branches for the after-school tutoring program

Church partners—$20,000 (all of these gifts are unrestricted)
- □ $10,000 from First Presbyterian downtown
- □ $4,000 from Risen Christ Lutheran
- □ $3,000 from Hallelujah Baptist
- □ $3,000 from the United Methodist Women at Wesley United Methodist

Individual donors—$20,000
- □ $10,000 from a special appeal letter to church members to fund the summer program for youth (average gift $50)
- □ $5,000 from the year-end appeal letter directed at church members (average gift $100)
- □ $2,500 from a major donor to cover the cost of new computer equipment for the computer lab
- □ $2,500 from a major donor, unrestricted funds

Special Events—$10,000
- □ $5,000 from the steak fry and silent auction

- ☐ $3,000 from pledges to the annual walk-a-thon
- ☐ $2,000 from cookie sales at Christmas Walk in the Park

Start with the People in Your Church

Several years back, I wrote *Winning Grants to Strengthen Your Ministry* (Alban Institute, 2002), so when I say at my seminars that church fund-raising efforts ought to start by asking church members to give, people often respond, "Don't tell us that—we came here to hear about grant writing!"

I think it is especially important with community ministry efforts to show that the sponsoring church community is financially supportive. Foundation funders might ask: "If the people who developed this thing won't give to it, why should we?" It's a good question, and any money you raise from church members for your work can help to leverage funding from outside your church.

I once worked on a fund-raising program at a church that was raising money for camp scholarships. An eight-year-old boy came up to me after the service and said, "Here is my allowance for this week—50 cents—I want to help send kids to camp!" You better believe I told that story to the largest foundation in the state when they came for their site visit. That foundation gave $50,000, and the little boy gave 50 cents. Both donations were needed that year to send kids to camp.

To raise money from church members, keep these rules of thumb in mind:

1. *Always schedule fund-raising appeals; don't make "asks" off the cuff.* You will undoubtedly be sharing the fund-raising year with a number of other appeals to the congregation, so be sure you coordinate the scheduling of your "ask" with everything else that is happening at church. Also, spontaneous requests for money may make it hard to maintain a positive relationship with the pastor and other church staff.

2. *Even if multiple appeals are happening at the same time, coordinate the different efforts.* In one of my church jobs, congregants were asked to give to three different special appeals at the end of the year:
   - ☐ Christmas food baskets and Christmas gifts for families from the community, distributed through the food shelf run by the church

□ The trustees' offering that helped fund special "fix-it" projects or equipment needs around the church

□ And my appeal—for the nonprofit connected to the church—to fund the health clinic, tutoring program, computer learning center, and a variety of other community-focused programs

We decided to combine our efforts by making a joint announcement from the pulpit three Sundays in a row (each group took one Sunday). We put an insert in the bulletin with all three appeals on it, we each sent out a separate mailing to the congregation, and then we reminded people each Sunday that they had three opportunities to give—a real choice—and that they could give to one, two, or all three! This joint appeal was well-received, and coordinating our efforts helped bring clarity, not confusion, to the congregation.

3. *Be clear about why you are making a special appeal.* People may ask why you are asking for a special gift when they already put a tithe or offering in the plate each week. Many churches don't communicate well with their congregations about what is in the church budget and what isn't—this can be an opportunity to educate people about the larger budget picture for the church. Also explain what the funding will support in as specific terms as you can. (Refer again to Model 1: "Donate Goods or Money.")

Building Relationships with Individual Donors

By focusing mainly on grant writing, ministries might neglect the development of an individual donor base, but individuals can provide some of the best funding for your ministry. Individual donors are often more loyal than grant funders, giving over a period of many years. Foundations and corporations tend to switch their focus and move on every few years, but if you cultivate your individual givers and build relationships with them, they may be with you long after grant funding expires. Moreover, the size of their donations may increase over time—this is much less true of grant funders. And in my experience, it is also true that individuals are more likely to give unrestricted gifts—money that can be used in any way you see fit.

So how do you go about developing an individual donor program? Here are a few best practices to try:

- *Approach people with some connection to your ministry first.* It may be tempting to approach the really rich strangers you see in the news, but in reality, you will be much more successful if you think about the people who are "nearby" your ministry work where there is a personal connection or some knowledge of the ministry. If you haven't already approached them, church members fall into this category. Volunteers in your program may also be good candidates for an ask—they have already demonstrated their commitment by giving their time; maybe money will follow. Friends, colleagues, and family members of people in your ministry (board, staff, and volunteers) are also people who are "nearby" who could potentially be asked to make a gift.
- *Meet face-to-face with potential major donors.* You might decide to send out fund-raising letters one or more times per year to some of your donors or "prospects," but consider having personal meetings with people who give (or might give) larger gifts to your ministry. What is considered "larger" varies between ministries—for your group it might be $100 or $250, while for others it might be well into the four or five figures.
- *Host a tour or site visit.* There is no substitute for getting potential donors on-site to see with their own eyes the program you are asking them to support. Some programs don't lend themselves to this kind of a visit—if there are confidential things being shared by clients, for example (as in a treatment or counseling program). In that case, you might invite some volunteers or "graduates" of the program who are willing to speak about their experiences at a meeting with the donor.
- *Send the right "asker."* Who asks for the gift can make a big difference in the outcome of the solicitation. The best "asker" is someone who is known and respected by the donor and who is currently an enthusiastic supporter of your organization. Lacking someone like that, you might think about someone with whom the donor would have something in common—they went to the same school or church,

for example, or they enjoy the same hobbies or work in the same field.

- *Ask for a specific amount.* Telepathy doesn't work with donors—you will have to tell them what you want! Decide how much to ask for before you have your meeting, and then ask. You can make sure you are in the right ballpark of an ask by doing some research on donors ahead of time. Study up on their line of work, the type of position they hold, involvement with other nonprofits, and what they give to those organizations.

- *Have good written materials.* Having a good one- or two-page summary of what you are doing is invaluable when meeting with individual donors. Most donors don't want to be inundated with paper or given a copy of your DVD. They just want to hear, in as concise a way as possible, about these four things:

  1. What you are doing. Describe your program or project in detail—who it is for, where and when it is, what is offered, who is partnering with you. If the "ask" is to help you reach further and expand your program, describe briefly the current status of the program and then flesh out your dream, including specific details where you can.

  2. The results of your efforts. Outcomes, yet again! Tell what difference your efforts will make in the world in as concrete terms as possible. Write down if kids graduated from high school because of your work, if people got jobs or housing, or if the overall health of your community improved.

  3. The estimated cost. Include a brief project budget as a part of your document.

  4. Opportunities for them to give. Lay out on the page a few specific ways donors can give—specific amounts of money required to underwrite a program or staff position, for example, or funds needed for capital improvements. Donors will often look at a list like this and pick out the one that best meets their interests and ability to give. Also, consider the wisdom or expertise the donor could lend your effort: Could you use help developing a strategic plan or advice on how to approach other

major donors? Sometimes donors will give more if they are asked to come in close to the organization and help in more hands-on ways.

■ *Follow-up.* Many gifts come after multiple meetings with a donor, so don't give up after the first meeting just because you don't leave with a check. Some donors like to spend time getting to know an organization and the people in it before making a gift—so multiple meetings are in order. Others like to jump in with both feet and volunteer so they can get a better sense of what the program is all about. People like this might make their first gift after volunteering for a while. An important part of follow-up is sending the donor what they ask for after the meeting—more written information about the program, a brochure, a budget, or a financial report, for example.

Finding Grant Funding

There isn't space in this book to fully cover all of the aspects of seeking grant funding, but I can offer a few thoughts on strategies to increase your success rate. Keep in mind that grant funding is a competitive process, with fewer dollars and more grant seekers in the mix than was the case a few years ago. It is not unusual for grant funders to fund somewhere in the range of 5 to 30 percent of the proposals they receive, so you will probably receive mostly nos and a few yeses. I am always clear about that up front so people don't give up after the first few nos.

Also, it is important to note that there are some ministries that may not be grant fundable at all. If you are working on something that few (or maybe no) grant funders in your area support, you will need to find support elsewhere. Here in the Twin Cities where I work, there used to be little funding for programs for seniors; now some funders are beginning to head into that area. And there used to be a great deal of funding for immigrant and refugee programs; now there is very little. Funding patterns shift over time, and certain areas of service are more popular with funders than others.

Here are some helpful strategies to get you started in your pursuit of grant success:

- Research funders carefully and choose to apply only to those that fit with what you are trying to do. Most funders post guidelines on their websites, as well as a list of organizations they have supported most recently. Choose the funders that seem to fit best with what you are trying to do; avoid those that don't seem like a fit. Shoot for a short list of funders—maybe five or ten rather than fifty.

- Articulate clear outcomes for your programs and outline how you will measure them. See "Measuring Success in Your Ministry" in Part Three on how to develop outcomes.

- Describe a clear design for your program, identifying where it is, who is served, what is being offered, who is involved (staff, volunteers, and partners), what the intended results are (those outcomes again), and how much it will cost.

- Keep your request concise and to the point. Many grant funders will ask for about five to seven pages of grant narrative, meaning you won't be able to be long-winded about any one aspect of your program or organization. The largest section of the proposal should be the program description—don't skimp on details there. (See "Elements of a Typical Grant Proposal" opposite.)

- Call foundation staff once you have reviewed the funder's guidelines (unless it explicitly states not to call). Keep your conversation short and to the point and focus on a few key issues, such as running your idea by the funder to get feedback, asking about an appropriate amount to ask for, and clarifying anything about the guidelines that is unclear to you.

- Pay attention to deadlines. Many funders have explicit calendar deadlines, though some accept proposals on an ongoing basis. If there is a deadline and you miss it, your proposal will likely not be considered. Deadlines are typically posted on a funder's website.

- Most corporate funders send grant dollars where their employees are involved as volunteers (often your grant won't even be considered unless you have an employee involved with you). So make sure you know where your board members, volunteers, and donors work so they can put in a good word for you when you submit your proposal.

Elements of a Typical Grant Proposal

Your state or region may have a "common grant application"—a format and list of questions that are used by many funders in your area. Look up the trade association for funders in your area, and you may well find the common grant application for your state or region on that website. Look at the Giving Forum website (www.givingforum.org) for a complete list of statewide and regional funder organizations.

Generally, most corporations and foundations will request the kinds of information covered below in a grant proposal. Special requests for capital funding or research dollars or for especially large requests may need to include information beyond this list. Read the guidelines for each foundation carefully to determine what needs to go in your proposal.

History of Your Organization

Funders typically want to know a bit about the history of your organization or program before they will consider funding you. This is the section of the proposal where you include your mission statement, a short description of how the organization or program was launched, and a list of your recent accomplishments. I like to write this up as a sequence of "increasing success." Even if you started small (or are still small), there are steps you took along the way that show that you know what you are doing and can actually deliver something to the community. So this section in a grant proposal that describes the development of an after-school program for youth might read like this:

- Parents in the neighborhood talked to the pastor about the need for after-school programming [shows the pastor is approachable and trusted].
- Church staff and lay leaders convened a meeting with neighborhood residents (including youth) to discuss what a program could look like [shows your church values the opinions of residents].

- Church staff and lay leaders designed a program based on community feedback, setting aside some funds from the church budget and space in the church building so that the new program could begin [shows the church values the program and the community enough to devote resources to it].

- The program began by offering one evening a week of programming. An increasing number of youth began participating, with fifteen to start, thirty after six months, now growing to fifty youth today. In response to the larger number of participants, staff and volunteers developed a wide range of activities youth can participate in—arts, sports, academics, and one-on-one mentoring [shows you have the ability to design and deliver a quality program that is multi-faceted and age specific].

- Grant funding was secured from First Corp so that the program could expand to three days a week. A part-time coordinator was hired with grant funding to oversee the expansion of the program and to recruit additional youth to participate. Two additional church partners were recruited, and they provided twenty new volunteers to help with tutoring [shows that your church can secure needed resources, plan ahead, and grow to meet needs].

Needs and Issues in the Community

Document why it is that your program or ministry is needed. You could use formal study data or statistics that describe a problem or need in your community. Census data, for example, might show the low high school graduation rate or high unemployment rate in your community. Universities in your area might conduct community needs assessments, or the United Way or a local foundation might send researchers out to assess access to early childhood education, the quality of health care, or why kids get involved in youth gangs, just to name a few issue areas.

You could also use informal data in this section of your proposal—things you know to be true about your community because you observed them yourself or because people in the neighborhood told you. You could conduct your own surveys or focus groups with residents or program participants, or simply begin to take note of comments that people make to you. I once worked for a church that had a food shelf, and we learned a great deal about which government programs were being cut or changed based on what people were requesting from us, as well as on how they looked when they came in. Changes in the Medicaid program, for example, meant that some people weren't able to receive medication they needed, so they looked sicker than they had before. We learned to ask about it when we noticed changes like this.

Description of Programs Offered by the Organization

Document all of the services and programs your church currently provides to the community. These could be both formal and informal programs and also ones that happen seasonally, like a Christmas store or health fair. Think hard about every way your congregation currently touches the community—sometimes churches leave out things they are doing because no one refers to the activity as a program or because it is something that doesn't require money or staff.

I have worked with several church-based preschools, for example, that had well-documented programs and outcomes for their children's programs, but somehow they didn't "count" all of the work they were doing with parents. Staff were putting a lot of time into helping parents get connected to housing and jobs, but because this work wasn't designated as a formal program, it didn't make it onto the list. They needed to count that work too when they were documenting their programs.

Description of the Program

This is the place to get as specific as you can about the program you are asking the funder to support. This section of the proposal should be close to half or even more of the length of the entire proposal, so don't skimp on details here! Sometimes funders complain to me that groups write a novel about their history and then just a few lines about the program they want funded. It should be the reverse! These are the kinds of details to include in your program description:

- *Target audience.* Who is the program for? What are the characteristics of this group and why do they need the program?
- *Where and when the program will be held.* Describe the location and why you chose it as well as the schedule for the program. How often does it occur and when?
- *What is being offered.* Describe your program content. What is being offered to participants?
- *Who is involved in offering the programming.* Tell whether paid staff or volunteers will be involved in delivering the program. Describe briefly the titles and duties of each key staff person and volunteer.

Model 6: "Develop a Ministry Program" includes more detail on what should be in your program design. Details of your design ought to be reflected in your grant proposal.

Collaborative Partners

Foundation and corporate funders want to know that you are maximizing your expertise and resources by collaborating with strategic partners. When you partner, you demonstrate that you are connected in the community, committed to not duplicating efforts, and making good use of your resources by focusing on what you do best. Usually this aspect of the proposal will include a list of your key collaborative partners with a short description (a sentence or two) of how you work with that partner. If you are a partnering church (see pages 144–146) with a whole boatload of partners, pick the five or ten groups that are your strongest, most engaged partners, or group them according to category, like this: "Church partners—ten different churches including Mount Olivet, St. Joseph's, and Holyoke Baptist provide over a hundred volunteers and contribute food to the food shelf every month." Your description of collaborative partners should be less than a page.

Evaluation Criteria

How will results be measured? This is one of the most important sections of your proposal, and funders tend to take a very close look at what is written here. It is the answer to that question again: What changes in the world because of your work? You can divide outcomes into long-term, intermediate, and short-term (more immediate). See pages 159–174 for ideas on developing and measuring outcomes.

Qualifications of Key Staff Members

Document the qualifications of your top two or three staff members, and be sure to include volunteers who are in leadership positions. Many churches I work with would include the pastor in this section, a key staff member who is involved in overseeing or operating the program, and possibly a key volunteer who has significant responsibility in the program. Qualifications should include educational credentials and work experience but may also include volunteer service.

Seeking Funding from Other Churches

In addition to pursuing funding through grants and individual donors, don't forget that many church congregations also give financially to ministries throughout the community, usually through a missions or outreach committee. Here are just a few tips on seeking funding from churches.

Think Denominationally and Beyond

Denominational affiliation still matters in how congregations decide to distribute their local missions dollars. Here in the Twin Cities, there are a number of larger, more prosperous churches that take a keen interest in smaller churches of their own denomination located in communities of high need. Volunteers from the larger churches are mobilized to these "urban outposts" to lend a hand but also to learn more about city life, youth, people of different ethnicities, and a variety of other issues. So if you want to seek funding from churches, think first about those congregations in your own denomination that might take a special interest in what you are doing.

That said, many congregations fund ministries outside their own denomination as well. These churches are usually less concerned about whether the Lutheran, Presbyterian, Baptist (you fill in the denominational blank here _____) banner is waved high and just want to connect with effective ministries that are making a real difference. I have noticed too that churches of different denominations may partner together because they have a particular theological bent—evangelical congregations in the mainline denominations, for example, or charismatic congregations from a variety of denominations.

Money Follows Relationships

In their missions giving, churches have become much more like corporations. Just as companies have long given where their employees are involved, congregations are increasingly inclined to give money to ministries and organizations where their members are involved as volunteers. So it is much less common now to simply go meet with a missions committee at a church and walk away with a check. Churches are focusing their funding on places where they can have more multifaceted relationships—such as the collaborations described in Model 3. So a church that gives you ministry money might also want to do some of the following:

- Send a person or two to sit on a board or advisory board connected to your ministry.
- Send their church members over to your place for tours so more people can learn about the community and your ministry.
- Mobilize volunteers from their church to work on a variety of tasks at your ministry. Just be sure that you can place the influx of people in helpful and accessible jobs. (See Model 2.)
- Help out with capital needs/physical repairs.
- Secure equipment or supplies that you need.

Application Processes Vary

The application process for funding can vary widely between congregations. Some just want you to jot down a page or two about what it is that you are doing. Some churches have detailed forms that are even more complex than those required by some foundations. Once you have submitted your application, you may be asked to come and present to the missions committee or local outreach board at the church. These meetings are almost like site visits with a foundation. Be prepared to tell the story, emphasize results/impact, and describe how the resources and people of their church will make a difference. You should also be prepared to talk about how a partnership can extend beyond their financial contribution—how their volunteers can get plugged into your ministry, for example.

Other Types of Funding

Funding doesn't have to be limited to grants, individuals, and churches. Here is a short list of other places you might look for funding:

Government grants. State, local, and federal funds may be available for a variety of programs, including early childhood education, housing, and health. Connect with opportunities through your own government officials (city council members, state and federal representatives, and senators) and be sure you can meet the reporting requirements before applying.

Local businesses. Small businesses in the neighborhood where your church is located could provide small financial gifts or in-kind donations. I have had particular luck in garnering support from small businesses for events—things like silent auction donations, prizes, and food.

Service clubs or fraternal organizations. Groups such as the Lions Club, Rotary, Jaycees, or VFW might provide funding as well. Some sororities and fraternities conduct major fund-raising campaigns and have a strong focus on community service. This is particularly true among African American sororities and fraternities. Many of these groups like to underwrite something specific—a piece of equipment, a van, camp scholarships, or something else.

Professional or trade associations. Your local bar association or medical association, for example, might offer support as well. Groups like this may be organized by affinity—I know of several focused on women ("women in management," "women in marketing") and African Americans (African American accountants and financial professionals). These groups are often particularly interested in getting their members engaged in community service. The bar association might help start a legal clinic, or an association of financial professionals might provide free financial management classes to the people in your community.

Neighborhood associations or block clubs. Depending on how your city government disburses funds, your neighborhood association or block club may serve as a funding "hub" for a variety of dollars. If they receive a larger grant, they may be looking to contract with groups like yours to actually develop and implement programming focused on health, youth development, crime prevention, or some other cause. So it is good to be connected with your neighborhood leaders so you can be informed of opportunities like this that arise.

Other larger nonprofits. Some of the larger nonprofits in your community may be looking to subcontract with smaller organizations to deliver services. They may also be willing to include collaborative partners in funding proposals. If your church or ministry is small, a larger nonprofit may have the fund-raising and management capacity to draw in large grants that your group could be a part of.

Fund-Raising: An Every-Week-of-the-Year Proposition

I talk to many, many people engaged in fund-raising every year, and my main advice is this: Keep at it! I think fund-raising is an every-week-of-the-year activity. The groups that are most successful at it are working on it all the time, and they don't give up just because they get a few nos along the way. Before you begin, it may be helpful to develop a calendar of fund-raising activities throughout the year—grant deadlines, special events and the preparation time for them, meetings with individual donors, and special mailings. With your work plotted out on a year-long timeline, you can avoid putting off fund-raising activities until later in the year and having everything pile up at the year's end, making it very difficult to meet your fund-raising goals.

Doing Community Ministry in the Small Church

Sometimes I interact with small congregations that assume that any significant community ministry effort is beyond their reach. They often keenly feel their limitations as they work to keep internal church programs (like a youth ministry) going with limited staff and volunteers—so how would they ever engage with the community in any significant way?

With the right approach, it is possible for a small group of people to make a big impact. It will take focus and clarity about what you are trying to accomplish, but the small ministry can make a big impact in the world through partnerships, creative use of resources, and a focus on relational ministry.

Integrating community ministry efforts into other ministries at your church is also possible. Some churches make community ministry a key component of youth group activities, mobilizing youth to a variety of service sites throughout the year. Or you might consider adding a service component to your next women's or men's ministry event.

Unique Strengths of Small Congregations

Small congregations have some unique strengths that can result in strong and effective community ministry programs. Because you are small, you may also be more disciplined about not "biting off more than you can chew." Identifying just one thing to focus on (tutor kids at the local public school, collect diapers, sponsor a community garden) may well help you be more successful, as you will have clear outcomes in front of you to work toward. I think sometimes there's a temptation for larger churches to make ministry efforts bigger and more complex than they need to be. Internal ministry programs may have many bells and whistles, so we need to do that with the work in our community as well—right? Wrong! Sometimes simpler is just what the community needs.

Another advantage to being small is that your church may be better at relational ministry than larger churches, and it is the relationships that you can build with the people in your community that will make the greatest impact. People who are drawn to attend smaller churches are often there because of the "family" feel—in your small congregation you can really get to know each other, go deep in your relationships, and bear one another's burdens. A pastor of a rural congregation in West Virginia told me that his small church is "a place of gathering, celebration, and common community. We still celebrate each person's birthday here!" Carrying that affinity for relationship into the community may well help you make a greater impact than if you brought hundreds of volunteers or thousands of dollars. Everything you've learned within your own congregation about really listening to one another and devoting time to relationships will bless your community in myriad ways.

Small churches often have no choice but to partner with others to carry out ministry, and partnership, if done well, can result in exponentially greater impact in the community. You aren't limited to the gifts and perspectives within your own congregation; you can seek others who make up the other half of what you don't have. Particularly when working on complex community issues when all kinds of people, expertise, connections, and resources are needed to move forward, the small church can really shine as one piece of a more complex partnership puzzle.

If you were going to work on the issue of gun violence in your community, for instance—a complex issue with many causes and impacts—the small church may be at the table with law enforcement, youth, parents, school administrators, youth development professionals, public officials, a community organizing group, other faith communities, and many other kinds of people and groups. Being almost "forced" to the table in this case could result in the needed multipronged strategy to address the issue, with the small church playing an important but clearly defined role in a much larger strategy.

In a small church, members may also feel a greater sense of ownership for the ministry. Without many paid staff, it really is up to church members to develop the vision and the plan, find partners, and enlist other church members to get involved. You can't just look around and say, "Pastor So-and-So is going to do that." In a small church, when you look around, you might only see yourself and a few of your friends. If you don't do it, no one else will! This strong ownership by lay leaders can help ministry be sustainable over the long term, long after paid staff members have moved on.

Finally, you may be better able to hold each other accountable for following through on ministry goals and commitments because you are small. If just a few of you are working on a project and two of you don't show up, it is pretty obvious who isn't holding up their end of the work! It is harder to be anonymous and go back on what you've agreed to. It is harder to give up when your friends are on your case!

Challenges Facing Smaller Congregations

The energy required for some small churches just to keep going may channel energy away from innovating new community ministry. If, for example, you are in a church that is so small that it is clear you will need to close soon, it will be hard for people to dream about the next chapter of your congregation's service to the community. Having continuous conversations about dwindling finances is draining, and there just may not be energy to focus on anything else.

Also, many small churches are in "single pastor" mode without other staff, meaning that there aren't "extra" staff resources to devote to ministry development, connecting in the community, raising money, recruiting volunteers, and all of the tasks involved in launching new efforts. One pastor told me, "I can't say, 'I'm going to go work on my sermon, would you please answer the phone or the doorbell.' There is no other paid staff! There is a lot of alone time. Without staff to support administrative efforts, I am interrupted all day long, and it is hard to complete tasks."

Sometimes small churches are made up mostly of people who have been at the church for a very long time, perhaps their entire lives. This may lead to what one pastor called "a sense of entitlement" on the part of longtime members. These longtime members may expect their opinions to be given more weight than that of newer members; they may feel they "deserve" leadership positions in the church; and they may be a loud voice for keeping things the way they have always been. Sometimes it even comes down to who gets to sit where in church and who gets to use the kitchen (or not). This entitlement culture may make it difficult for new people to enter the church, and it is new people who may be needed to bring new ideas and energy for new community ministry.

Making a church building welcoming for new ministry may be a challenge for smaller congregations. If you are small because your church is just starting out, you may be meeting in someone else's building for worship services, making it difficult to offer community ministry programming on-site. If you are small and your church has been around awhile, you might own a facility that needs repairs or reconfiguration. For congregations that are financially challenged and own a building, keeping the facility up often goes by the wayside in the interest of keeping on paid staff. So if your facility needs paint, new flooring and furniture, new fixtures including bathrooms, and cosmetic updates—or any of the above—it makes it harder to welcome in new groups and people.

Sometimes old church buildings aren't configured for new community uses. I have worked with several small churches in very large buildings that were built during the 1950s, when Americans were attending church in droves and Sunday schools were filled with children of all ages. The ten or twenty small second-floor Sunday school rooms made sense at the time, but they are limiting for a congregation that now needs accessible space for seniors or people with disabilities, or for a church that requires large multipurpose rooms to offer youth programming or health ministries.

Strategies for Being Successful

Small Is Beautiful

Some of the most successful community ministry programs are small and focused efforts that don't require a lot of money or people. Recently I have worked with several smaller churches that were developing partnerships with public schools. We started with a goal of recruiting just ten volunteers from each church, and they met that goal. Next people from the church started going into the school every week, learning about the needs of students, interacting with teachers and other staff, and making an impact by being faithful. So don't be frustrated if your plan for ministry isn't going to impact hundreds of people from the outset. A small group of people who are willing to keep at it can make a big difference!

Engaging in significant partnerships becomes even more important for the small congregation. It is possible that on your own you really don't have the people power and other resources to move forward into the community in a significant way. But with a partner you can multiply your efforts many times over. As outlined in Model 3, partners can provide space, staff, program expertise, funding, volunteers, use of equipment or supplies, and connections to other partners. Say you have a handful of volunteers from your small church who are willing to help in the community. Your partner pulls volunteers from many congregations, so now your church members are part of a larger effort. Your partner can provide training and other resources for volunteers, and then your volunteers can interact with many other people who share the same passion and bring a variety of ideas.

Permission to Explore New Gifts

Another helpful strategy when your church is small is to develop a "permission-giving" culture within your church. One pastor described this as "making hamburger out of your sacred cows." She said, "Just invite people in, and then say, 'Yes!' Let people explore your ministry, get a sense of it, and develop their own ways of helping. We think that to be good leaders we need to be directive, but I'm not sure it is the best way to lead. Instead, ask people what they are good at, what their gifts are. And let them decide how they would like to help. I say, 'So you're a belly dancer! Probably we won't have you dance during Sunday worship, but maybe you could offer exercise classes to the community.'"

Organizing ministry around the gifts of the people in your church is important in any congregation, but when you are small, it is also easier. There are many strategies for helping people find their spiritual gifts (some are outlined in "Finding a Fit between Church and Community" in Part One), but because people in your church probably know each other well, you may not need to pull out the spiritual gifts inventories. You can probably see with your own eyes what gifts are present in the people. You just have to be sure to tell one another! One pastor told me that pastors of small churches often see their churches through the lens "of all that we don't have," but he said that God continually draws him back to this question: "What are you doing with what you do have?" "People's gifts are infectious," he said, and allowing people to use their gifts has helped catalyze new ministry at his church.

Don't Be Shy

Be bold! Don't be afraid to ask for the resources you need. Depending on what you decide to do, you may not have all of the resources in your congregation to launch new ministry. You will need to ask for money outside your church, in-kind donations, and volunteers. Networking widely in your community with other churches, businesses, service clubs, and individuals will likely be an important part of your community ministry effort. As a small church, you will probably have to put aside any fear and shame you feel about asking for money or "stuff" and just get out there and ask!

St. John's United Church of Christ, Aurora, Illinois: Small Church with a Big Impact

St. John's United Church of Christ is a multiethnic church in Aurora, Illinois, that has about twenty people in worship on a Sunday morning. Congregants are low in financial resources (about 85 percent are unemployed, in low-paying service jobs, undocumented immigrants, or elderly) but high on enthusiasm for ministering in the community.

The congregation has developed four community ministry programs through partnerships and creative use of resources. Pastor Cyndi Gavin says that an important part of ministry development at her church has been to "reframe thinking." "Everyone measures success based on what happens in the Sunday service—how good the sermon was, the music, how many people were there. We have reframed this to be 'How many touches in the community does our church make each week?' We ask ourselves, how much healing happens in the community because of our church?"

Pastor Gavin began the process of ministry development by looking at needs assessments and studies conducted by other groups in her town. Resources from the local United Way, the county health department, and the Aurora Community Neighborhood Plans helped her see that there were high incidences of obesity and diabetes among people in the community, as well as a comparatively high infant mortality rate. Residents also identified the need for more summer programming for youth and more arts programming. Once she saw the "big picture" of community needs in the area, Gavin began meeting with agencies in the community—the women's shelter, the Salvation Army, a bilingual mentoring group, and many others.

Out of the community investigation process, the Mesa de María program was born—a cooking class and "table spirituality" for Latinas in the community who are pregnant or mothering/grandmothering children. The program offers healthy cooking classes that help families "change family eating habits and change the way they relate to food," according to Gavin. For example, participants are advised to use yogurt instead of lard when making tamales. After they work together to prepare the meal, women sit down at beautifully set tables with tablecloths and flowers. Gavin is convinced that when "women sit together at a beautiful table and eat lovingly prepared food slowly, they don't eat as much." The program has grown to include a focus on empowerment and instruction on stress relief, health, and money management.

St. John's also developed the Peace Players, a two-week summer camp for children focused on four components of peace—peace within, peace in my family, peace in the community, and peace on and with the earth. The program was developed in response to the community's expressed need for additional summer and arts programming. The camp is facilitated and directed by actors, artists, and a therapist, and the children actually create the performance showcase themselves. In the past, performances have included dance, pantomime, acting, singing, visual arts, and spoken word—all on the theme of peace.

A diabetic foot clinic is done in pilot partnership with Wound Care Education Institute. It is held three times a year at the church. Certified nurses check the foot structure of people with diabetes and then make recommendations about the types of socks and shoes they should wear. Special therapeutic shoes for diabetics are given to people who need them. Glucose screening tests are conducted on-site, and participants receive glucometers and a list of programs in the community that provide services to people with diabetes. The program has served as a pilot and model for other groups to start diabetic foot clinics around the country. The Wound Care Education Institute presents the story of St. John's at a national conference each year.

St. John's has also developed the Community Clothes Closet with a partner organization that helps families transition out of homelessness. The program originally happened only at Christmastime but is now open once a month, and appointments are scheduled for families that have an emergency need for clothing. In a recent month, the clothing closet served 103 families from the community and distributed 2,200 items of clothing.

Every year the church partners with Operation Warm Coats for Kids to purchase three hundred or more brand-new coats for the school district's most vulnerable children. Working with local public schools to distribute the coats to students, St. John's has built ongoing relationships with the school social workers. The church's clothing closet provides emergency clothing for children, and the school social workers solicit donations of supplies needed for the closet, such as plastic hangers. In 2012, for the first time, toys were distributed at the church at Christmastime. Women and girls who volunteered to help with the clothing donations had the idea to conduct a toy drive in their neighborhood and showed up one day with two truckloads of toys! "We had dreamed of having a toy closet; we just didn't know where we could get the toys. All of a sudden they appeared!" said Pastor Cyndi.

The clothing closet has become a real magnet for community volunteers, and some are showing up occasionally at St. John's for church. A large number of youth are volunteering—some come two and three times a week and bring their homework! Some of the youth have started getting involved in the church, participating in a drama one Sunday morning about Ruth and Boaz, and helping with candle lighting for Advent. "They come to help us, but they stay for moral support and to share their stories," Pastor Cyndi said.

To community members, shopping day at the Community Clothes Closet has become more than a chance to meet a basic need. Participants tend to stay more than an hour, talking with one another and the volunteers, eating, and watching their children create art at the children's table. It is a place where people can express their needs and build relationships.

Keep Going

Small churches are all too aware of the challenges facing their ministries—the limited funds, only a small number of church members, and a building that needs work. Even in the face of such challenges, however, your small church may be able to start some very powerful community ministries. Take stock of what you do have rather than what you don't have, and build on those assets. Be creative about finding partners, raising money, and securing in-kind donations. And most importantly, keep going.

How does Pastor Cyndi keep going in the midst of the challenges facing her congregation? She says: "I can keep doing this because of the gratitude of the people. People say they think this church is a safe place, where they can breathe freely and feel loved. People from the community say, 'We see you here at all hours, we see the light on, so we know that you love our community.' Moms from the community bring all of their children in to see me—they all hug me, and I sit with the moms. They speak to me in Spanish, which I can't understand, but we look at each other. I sit and hold their hands while they tell me about their lives, and sometimes they cry. Who could not be transformed by that much genuine, open love every day?"

Overcoming Obstacles, Celebrating Victories

Developing new ministry isn't usually a smooth road with no bumps. Think of yourselves as pioneers on a barely worn path in the wilderness. It can take a long time to get from the scarcely noticeable trail through the grass (your first thoughts and dreams about a ministry) to the four-lane superhighway (a fully implemented plan with staff and resources in place). People who have been at this for a while can tell you that it can take years and years, even decades to fully develop a ministry dream.

Encountering obstacles is a part of the journey and can lead to stronger ministry as you are forced to reevaluate what this ministry is all about and renew your commitment to the work. Here are some common obstacles you may face as you move forward into the community, and some strategies for responding to them.

Obstacle 1: We Don't Have Enough Money

When church budgets are crunched, community ministries might end up on the chopping block along with everything else. However, it is possible to do meaningful community ministry with no or very little money. Significant involvement of volunteers often provides the greatest cost savings, helping congregations forgo the need for paid staff. If the budget is a concern, think through how you could use volunteers to do direct service work, such as running youth programs and teaching job skills, as well as administrative work, such as recruiting and training volunteers, buying supplies, and setting up and tearing down equipment for an event. Volunteers can also take charge of marketing and communications, fund-raising efforts, and special events.

Seeking in-kind donations of supplies and equipment can provide additional cost savings. Over the years, I have secured in-kind donations of books, computers, office furniture, food, toys, legal and accounting services, athletic equipment, clothing, and baby supplies—just to name a few. Securing donated space where you can hold ministry activities can also be a help. If you can't meet in your church, check out other churches, community centers, schools, your local park, libraries, or government offices. Even a local business might provide space free of charge.

You might decide to develop several different scenarios for how community ministry programs could be operated, depending on how much funding is available. Maybe the ideal scenario would be for your program to have two paid staff running it. But what would the program look like if you could just afford one paid staff member and use volunteers to fill in the rest? Or you may want to develop several scenarios about the number of people served or the number of hours your program is open each week, for example.

Of course, you can always look at ways to generate funding outside the church budget. Donated income from grants, individual donors, and other churches is a possibility (see "Securing Funds for Your Ministry" in Part Three). Also, some churches generate earned income through their community ministries by selling goods or services—for example, sales of bikes and equipment at your nonprofit bike shop, rental income from your affordable housing program, or income from the farmers' market where your church sells produce raised in your community garden.

Obstacle 2: We Don't Have Enough People

Smaller churches often face the challenge of having just a handful of people who do everything in the church. Particularly in churches with just one paid staff member, parishioners are often called upon to do just about everything—lead worship, serve communion, provide hospitality, work with children and youth, visit the sick, teach, fix what is broken, and clean up after everyone has gone home (and that is not a complete list!). How could community ministry be added when everyone's plate is already so full?

You will still need a few people (perhaps as few as three to five) to champion and organize a community ministry effort, but partnership with other congregations and agencies in your community becomes a critical strategy if your church struggles with this obstacle. Think of your congregation as a possible catalyst for an effort that would involve many other kinds of people and groups. I frequently work with "David-sized" churches that have a "Goliath-sized" impact in the community because they had a small group of dedicated people who were willing to serve sacrificially. When people outside your church observe this sacrifice and commitment, they may be inspired to sacrifice in their own ways, giving time and money, and helping your church network with other groups in the community.

One small congregation I have worked with runs a café in the community center where the church is located. The woman who runs the café is a dedicated volunteer who oversees the operation of the Café and also mentors and trains young people from the community who serve as employees. She also trains and equips volunteers, interacts with church partners, and dreams up new program ideas. She is a fixture in the building, and her extraordinary commitment to this (unpaid) work draws all kinds of people in—new volunteers, community partners, churches that want to help, and donors who show up with financial donations because they can see the great difference this small church is making in the community.

Obstacle 3: We Don't Know What Our Community Needs

Sometimes feeling in the dark about the community surrounding your church can be a real obstacle to moving forward. And sometimes this concern is not expressed as such because it is difficult to essentially say, "We don't know anything!" or "We're ignorant about our community!" Instead, people might say things like "Where would we even start?" or "We don't have any idea about the kind of programs we could offer." Meeting the neighbors is a critical step if your church struggles with this obstacle. You might even set a goal of involving a larger group of people in the process of getting out and meeting with people, creating a greater sense of competence within the congregation about community issues. This process can reenergize your congregation as people begin to envision how your church could engage in meaningful ways in the community. Church members might even come back with a picture or vision of what is needed. What if, for example, they met immigrants and refugees and saw their struggles—not only for the basics (food and housing), but also their need for friendships in a new land? Out of that might come a picture of how the congregation could engage—not just as providers of "stuff," but as caring neighbors and friends. It may take some effort to get your church to agree to a Meet the Neighbors process, but if they agree to do it, it will be well worth the effort.

Obstacle 4: Community Ministry Distracts from Core Ministries

In churches, we often pit ministries against each other. We set up false dichotomies: "We can either have strong adult education *or* strong youth ministry" or "We can either have strong programs inside our church to serve us *or* we can go into the community and serve 'them.'" By being creative, churches can do both. Community ministry can be incorporated into almost any ministry in the church. There isn't any reason community ministry couldn't become a focus of your youth ministry—for example, incorporating community service activities into your weekly youth night on a regular basis. And for adult spiritual formation, how about a study of "hunger" in the Bible and then a study of hunger in your community, culminating in a planning process for how your church could get involved in helping alleviate hunger in your area. Youth could be invited to participate in the study and planning process as well. Community ministry programs present great opportunities for the generations to get together. So rather than expending energy planning social events or outings for youth, young families, baby boomers, and seniors in the same month, why not combine forces and do something for the community? We might not all like the same social activities (snowboarding vs. visiting a playground vs. going out to dinner vs. going to a book club), but we could probably all get together for a community workday at the local park, where people of all ages pick up trash, install playground equipment, and plant flowers.

Obstacle 5: Key (Vocal) People Oppose Our Involvement

If you have a few vocal people in your church who are opposing new vision for community ministry, here are a few things you can try. First, try to involve them or give them a role in the process of forming new ministry. Think about what their primary objections are, and get them engaged in resolving that issue or at least gathering more information. For example, if they insist that the church really doesn't know anything about the community, see if they would serve on the Meet the Neighbors team. Getting out into the community and seeing firsthand both the good and challenging things that are happening has helped to light a fire under many a skeptic.

Another good strategy: connect with the people in question directly to make sure you understand their concerns, and then stay connected to assure them that those concerns are being addressed. Once when I was working on restarting a church-based nonprofit, an older gentlemen in the congregation kept raising objections to some of the details—forming a separate board for the nonprofit, in particular. He expressed concern about the possibility that the nonprofit would head in a different direction than the church, something that had happened with the community center down the street years before. I met with him individually several times to make sure that I understood his concerns and then made sure that those were addressed in specific ways at every congregational meeting we held about the process.

Finally, if these are the same vocal people who always seem to oppose anything new, it may take intervention by your pastor or other appointed church leaders to get them to stop. Sometimes a strategic conversation with "loud" people asking them to tone it down or hold on to their objections for a while can help. After all, if a majority of church members are committed and involved, the vocal minority may be assured that their concerns have been heard—and that it is now time to move on.

Obstacle 6: Our Past Behavior
Inspires Suspicion in the Community

Some churches may have trouble engaging in new community ministry because past community interactions didn't go so well. Maybe your church started a community ministry and couldn't follow through; maybe you made promises you couldn't keep. Or perhaps people from your congregation interacted with the community in ways that were harmful or negative. My family once attended a church that didn't make the shift when the community became multiracial in the 1950s. African American visitors were greeted at the door by an usher who said, "We think you want the Baptist church down the street." Now the church is proudly multiethnic, but it took a long time for the people in the community to forget what had happened before.

If your church has these kinds of failures in its past, the "Meet the Neighbors" step becomes even more important. You will not only be learning about your community but also building new relationships and healing old ones, maybe rebuilding some burned bridges as well. Your listening process ought to include questions like these: "What have your past interactions with our church been like?" and "How can we make it different this time?"

You might also want to consider checking back with community members a few times as you develop your community ministry strategy, inviting feedback and being willing to make changes based on what people tell you. Reconnecting during the process can also give you the chance to inform people about the concrete ways you are moving forward, building confidence in the community that the idea you are developing will actually come to fruition.

Obstacle 7: We Can't Get Our Act Together

Some churches just seem to be administratively challenged. (I won't say disorganized!) If you look at the recent history of your church and see a lot of "fits and starts" (mostly fits), then you may be struggling with this obstacle. A common picture would be that someone in the congregation has a great idea for ministry, everyone seems to be coming together around it, and then there is poor follow-through. Volunteers are not called back, events and meetings are not scheduled, and pretty soon this great idea seems to have fallen off the map. If this is your church, here are a few things you can do:

- *Pursue one of the less complicated models.* Maybe gathering goods (Model 1) would work well for you, or perhaps you could try the public policy model with a strong partner. Models 6 and 7 may be ones to avoid.
- *Enlist administratively gifted members of the congregation.* You need them! These are the people who can design systems and processes and then use those to implement the idea. Sometimes I find that the organized people have given up being involved because they are frustrated with the lack of follow-through. See if you can find them and let them have significant leadership roles in forming new initiatives.
- *Hire staff with organizational/administrative skills.* If you can find the resources, hiring someone even a few hours a week who can keep your plans moving along will be worth every dime. In the past, I have looked for someone who is a self-starter, who can see where the gaps are and fill them in with little prompting, accomplishing tasks such as arranging meetings, calling volunteers, communicating with outside partners, moving needed paperwork and getting important items on the meeting agenda.

Celebrating Victories

Don't forget to celebrate the victories along the way with your congregation. Starting new ministry efforts can be all-consuming, and it can be easy to forget to celebrate. Celebration sets a positive tone in the congregation and gets people focused on what has been accomplished (rather than on mistakes or failure). Also, success begets success—more people will be drawn into volunteering, giving, and participating in other ways as they see how your ministry idea is moving forward.

As you move forward, you might celebrate the following kinds of milestones in the development of new ministry. Even if these seem small to you, it is important to mark progress and keep people updated on how the new ministry is going. Consider moving into celebration mode when you can announce these sorts of things:

- We have trained and mobilized our volunteers [award certificates].
- We launched the program [ribbon cutting or similar].
- We held an event that was well-attended [photos/videos].
- We found a new community partner [introduce a representative of that partnership by highlighting what that partner brings to your ministry effort].
- We built relationships with people from our community who we didn't know before [invite them to participate when you communicate this to the congregation].

The last item, reporting on results, would be your evaluation results/measurement of program outcomes, such as:

- Our advocacy efforts helped ensure that an important piece of legislation passed.
- Our job training program resulted in X number of people getting jobs.
- Crime is down in our neighborhood because of the efforts of the block club network that our church sponsors.

You can highlight progress and successes through standard church communication channels:

- In written communication, such as the bulletin, newsletter, or email message
- Through a church-wide event such as a dinner or a party
- By featuring announcements or testimonials from the pulpit
- By holding a gathering in the community with church members and partners

In addition to these more standard methods of communication, think about some creative ways you might draw attention to your ministry success. Several groups I have worked with created a large visual object that was set in a prominent place in the church to draw attention. A giant cardboard turkey for your turkey drive? An interesting-looking bike for the opening of the bike shop? It should be something that is hard to miss in a hard-to-miss location.

"Kooky" announcements up front on a Sunday morning can also work if you don't overuse them. Find the most outgoing person in your congregation, who seems to have no shame doing something silly in public, and ask that person to do a chant or a cheer or a dance—whatever it takes to get people's attention. These really do work. I've been a part of some pretty memorable ones that people are still talking about!

Another interesting strategy is to give each person in the congregation an object they can take home to remind them of the work and the contribution they made. One small church I am working with made refrigerator magnets—small wooden dolls—to remind people in the church of the hunger needs in the community and the people they had helped through their efforts. This was years ago, and some of the magnets are still in place, reminding people every day of their church's commitment to the community.

Pause for a Success Break

Moving forward on community ministry often takes so much continuous work that it is hard to pause for any reason, much less to celebrate successes. But make sure to pause. Even if you don't see much to celebrate, take time to identify where you *have* made progress over a period of time, and then highlight that for your congregation.

Starting new community ministry almost always involves some level of "failure"—things don't go the way you planned, so you have to restructure, reconfigure, or start again. If leaders in the church decide to focus on what has been accomplished rather than on what was disappointing about your new ministry endeavor, it will make all the difference in your ability to get the ministry started. Develop the habit of talking together about what is good and right about your community ministry efforts. This will help encourage your leaders and set the table for more success.

Conclusion

As I finish up this book, I am reflecting on two years of research into the topic of community ministry as well as my own work on the frontlines of ministry over a period of 20 years. Through all the bumps and bruises I have experienced myself and the difficult stories I have heard, I still believe that the church is in a unique position to make a real difference in communities. We are called to this work as Christians, gifted by God to do it, and (hopefully) blessed with a sense of determination that won't allow us to give up at the first evidence of setbacks.

I have seen the church make a miraculous impact in communities, usually when church members are passionate, thoughtful, and strategic in their work. I have watched children successfully prepare for kindergarten, addicts recover, teens graduate from high school, sick people become healed, and neighbors improve their neighborhoods—all because churches decided that it wasn't enough to sit inside the building and pour more resources into the congregation itself. These churches decided that ministry "out there" was just as important, if not more important, than the internal ministries of the church, so much so that they devoted time, money, energy, and people to the task at hand.

I hope reading this book has inspired you to do more in your community. I hope you have read about some models that you can use and have been encouraged by advice that rings true in your situation. My own ministry dream is that congregations would be courageous and strategic in serving their communities. Not content to do the least and the easiest, but willing to dream big, stretch themselves, and really *be* the Body of Christ to their neighbors. I believe the possibilities are limitless.

Recommended Resources

Justice and Mission Resources

Danielle Ayers and Reginald Williams. *To Serve This Present Age: Social Justice Ministry in the African American Church.* Judson Press, 2013.

Glynis LaBarre. *Learning Mission, Living Mission: Churches That Work.* Judson Press, 2012.

J. Alfred Smith Sr. *Speak until Justice Wakes: Prophetic Reflections from J. Alfred Smith Sr.* Judson Press, 2006.

Issue-Specific Resources

Brenda Branson and Paula Silva. *Violence among Us: Ministry to Families in Crisis.* Judson Press, 2008.

W. Wilson Goode, Charles E. Lewis Jr., and Harold Dean Trulear, editors. *Ministry with Prisoners and Families.* Judson Press, 2012.

Wilda K. W. Morris. *Stop the Violence! Educating Ourselves to Protect Our Youth.* Judson Press, 2001. Student book and leader guide are available.

Scott Sabin. *Tending to Eden: Environmental Stewardship for Today's Church.* Judson Press, 2010.

Ron Sider and Heidi Rolland Unruh, editors. *Hope for Children in Poverty: Profiles and Possibilities.* Judson Press, 2007.

Nonprofit Resources

Bryan W. Barry. *Strategic Planning Workbook for Nonprofit Organizations.* Fieldstone Alliance, 1997.

Anthony Mancuso. *How to Form a Nonprofit Corporation.* Nolo, 2011. A good resource for familiarizing yourself with the legal process. They advise you to do it yourself; I advise you to use an attorney.